I Don't Have the Answers

But I Do Have Some Questions

By King Charles Smith

King Charles Smith

I Don't Have the Answers,
But I Do Have Some Questions

ISBN-13:978-1720353249

Copyright 2018

Note: This book and publication contains strong and adult language or content.

All rights reserved. No part of this publication may be reproduced, distributed, or transmitted in any form or by any means, including photocopying, recording, or other electronic or mechanical methods without the prior written permission of the publisher or author, except for non-critical reviews and certain other noncommercial uses permitted by copyright law. For permission requests, write to the author, addressed "Attention: Permissions Coordinator," at the address below.

King Charles Smith
King Charles Productions

Website: http://www.kingcharlesproduction.com
Email: kingcharlesproductions@gmail.com

Published by
CRB Publishing
P.O. Box 201272, Arlington, TX 76006
(800) 718-2425

Printed in the United States of America

I Don't Have the Answers

But I Do Have Some Questions

By King Charles Smith

INSIDE THIS BOOK

SUBJECT & CHAPTER TITLE	PAGE
Ladies, when breaking-up with a man, do you want him to fight for your love…or move on?	7
Is it possible to have a long-distance relationship?	13
Your man had a hard-stressful day. What does he get when he gets home?	21
Men, the sex would be off the charts if she just stops……?	28
Your mate confesses to cheating; do you need to know with who and why?	34
Is a trans-woman still a man?	41
Can you be married and still lonely?	62
Do all men pay for sex one way or another?	70
Just Married! He's 19, and she's 44. Is age just a number?	78
Do all women look at another woman's butt?	91
Would you stay with your mate that has contracted HIV through a blood transfusion?	98
Is a man potentially on the DL if he likes and wants anal sex with his wife?	108
What's the difference between opinions and judging?	115
If a Man/Woman is Legally Separated, is it Wrong for Them to Date?	121
When he Proposes and doesn't Accept, is the Relationship Over?	130

About the Author

King Charles has lived life! Whether you consider his past "rosy" or "horrid", he lived it the way he understood it. From foster care, gangs, drug addiction and incarceration, he has been through literal hell. King Charles became caught up in a system that failed him; his home structure failed him, the streets failed him, plus an addiction that coerced him and yet failed him again. His past was intended to destroy him, but instead he has risen from the ashes and lives with passion for his new-found life.

He is blessed to understand that God has given him a new purpose on his journey and that is to inspire Kings and Queens! His message is to inspire in all areas of life. From marriage/dating, grief, gangs, drugs, molestation, broken homes, all topics where hope can be fostered into seemingly hopeless situations. To give inspiration to others that, they too, can live their own life again!

King Charles has a God-given talent which is his voice. Though untrained, yet perfected, King Charles is a radio personality who uses not only his voice, but his passion through the airwaves and through the heartbeats of people like you and I to make a change within ourselves, our family, and within our communities.

With his enormous following from his Facebook group he established in 2015, King Charles has grown his membership from a few dedicated members to more than 10,000 actively engaged members. Listen intently and you'll hear the same passion of life through the messages in this book.

King Charles Smith

CHAPTER 1

Ladies, when breaking-up, do you want him to fight for your love...or move on?

QUESTION: Ladies, when breaking-up, do you want him to fight for your love...or move on?

MG- No need in fighting for something we chose to walk away from. Fight before flight!

SA- First I must assure myself it's worth fighting for and evaluate it from all angles. I must look at what part I played in the break-up before throwing in the towel completely. This question needs to be more simplified......like how long the relationship was? Reasoning behind the breakup? I truly believe if someone wants to leave, let them go!

MC- Be wary of men who want to "stay friends " or stay on good terms...it's a trap

DB- Too old and wise for shenanigans. If I broke up with him he MUST move on and I will take all necessary measures to see that he does one way or another... His choice of how that will be.

DD- I want him to move on, as I will. I have remained friends with all but one of my ex-boyfriends. We all moved on to other relationships, but our friendships are solid (if they were really friends in the first place). Sometimes (many times) we are better friends. None of the current girlfriends feel threatened by me because they have met me and know the type of person I am. Life is too short.

BB- If the word Break up come to say from our heart. It's over. Because why is it in there? It a reason for everything.

I Don't Have the Answers, But I Do Have Some Questions

IM- I think everybody got away from the question. Truly for a man's point of view if you really loved a woman you break up you going to fight to get her back. I hear this lady's talking about just bye what the was the point in the first place. If you say bye you weren't in love anyway. Just saying.

RD- No because if you and him it must be a reason for the break up.

SK- JUST FOR FLATTERY. TRY & GET ME BACK!

EBAS- It's Depends on The Man and The Relationship.

BB- If we are good together, I want him to fight. But if it is bad, bye-bye, baby.

NM- It depends on the reason for breaking up. If he is a cheater, abuse me, or an opportunist to my funds....NO! LEAVE. If I feel like I'm unappreciated over time or neglected after I am telling him let's reignite the emotions that existed in the beginning of our relationship as a couple or stir up our complacent routine or get creative on keeping our union fresh! Yes, I would want him to put forth an effort to keep me. Or change my mind, cause my heart would be with him regardless. He just wouldn't know it because of the hurt I would feel he caused or inflicted on me from neglect.

TC- Move the F*%# on!

KING-ISMS

Love comes in many different shades of color. Whenever love exists between two individuals, it is -- at the very least -- slightly different than any love that existed before it, and any love that will exist after it. Love is created between two individuals, and just as no two individuals are the same, neither can the love between them be the same, however, love is still love. When we see it, we recognize it -- no matter how many shades lighter or darker it may be than anything we've previously experienced.

If I had to describe love in one sentence, I would describe it as such: Love is that which we believe worth fighting for.

How much we are willing to fight for it; how much we are willing to suffer for it and give up for it lets us know how true it really is.
The only love worth having is the one worth fighting for -- because anything short of that just isn't love.
If you aren't willing to fight for it, then you clearly don't want it enough.

It doesn't matter whether we're talking about life goals or lovers, if you aren't willing to fight for them, if you aren't willing to get your hands dirty, to go out of your way and try to hold on to them, then you just don't want them enough. And regardless of whether it's a goal or other, if you don't want it enough, then you don't deserve it.

People have many wants and urges. We often want more than is good for us -- and this doesn't change when it comes to attention or love. We're social gluttons of sorts. We want to be loved. We want to be taken care of. We want to feel like we've found our home. Which is great, except all those things we want do little more than build us a wider comfort zone. No one, and I mean no one, lives a happy life entirely inside his or her comfort zone. Finding someone worth fighting for drags you out of that zone and into a more eventful life.

The question is do you love this person enough to step out of your comfort zone and into the ring to fight for him or her? This goes beyond the male ego who just wants what is his. This is because he
knows who and what he has is one of a kind, something he can't just find anywhere else. And because of this he is willing to fight for it. He would never fight for something or someone he doesn't really care about, but because he loves you he will always be there to defend you or help you in any way he can.

Your Answer

CHAPTER 2

Is it possible to have a long-distance relationship?

QUESTION: Is it possible to have a long-distance relationship?

JE- It's hard to have a right here one, and you're talking about long distance!

GP- Not really. But I'm just speaking 4 ME. But I have known some people to do so.

KS- Yes, I truly do, QGB you and most people base their relationship off feelings instead of maturity sweetheart, feelings cast doubt and lingering questions.

QGB-Feelings cast doubt and lingering questions who brings with them baggage from past relationships, you're correct on that King

KS.-The maturity level that dares to handle the attempt of a long-distance relationship comes more with the consistency of reaching out; even more then if you lived in the same City. Not to the point of overindulging, but to spring up in surprise of sorts. Good morning quotes, just thinking thoughts of your poems, etc. But now that I think of it, these exact same gestures should be out forth regardless! Lol It does take a maturity, mindset if you will, to recognize and pull off this type of venture...Smiling

NT- Yes, I did most of my adult life and I married both women, we broke up when we lived together. Lol😊 true story.

DB- Yes, I could for a while because I fall in love with the internal of a man which could satisfy me for a while without being always able to have the external of the man in my presence to touch. However, I WILL eventually need and want both the internal and external of him... So, we will have to close the gap 💗

QGB- Absolutely Queen DB, this would need to be one of the first thing's discussed at the very beginning of the attempt to date long distance. Who would be willing to relocate if you decided to pursue this thing? It would need to be a temporary stint to even consider it to be worth it or not, I agree with you...Smiling

RB- Yes, if you're willing to move for Love. My son met his wife on line. 🖤 ❤️

MC- Yes. I was faithful to my ex when he was in the military and often gone...problems arose when he got back and started cheating. dumbass had a good alibi whilst he was gone...smsh!

RK- Negative because humans need touch and interaction on a up close and personal level.

RW- Yes, my son met his now fiancé on line, twelve years together. She moves here to be with him, they are so inseparable! They Both have very good careers.

CA- Relationships, regardless how we meet, start when we come together, does not the Scripture teach us, "A man shall leave his mother and father, cling unto his wife and become one flesh." We cannot remain truthful to someone miles away from us because we are not in a relationship; therefore, we can only deny ourselves until he or she comes home to us to join in a relationship.

KS- I disagree!

CA- I am sorry it took so long to respond to your not agreeing with what I said about relationships not starting until we get together, and I have no problem with that; however, you did not give nor explain why you disagree with it; I love to learn, and you might have a point, so share it, ok? First, my brother KS is a man lol, but respectfully answering your question simply by stating facts, you see fact of the matter is that maturity Absolutely has bases in *some "relationship" therefore it's wise to suggest that intimacy doesn't have to be tangible just on the guidelines of equal values as a whole (one) my brother. You see those who have a connection with God, God makes it clear that he wants us to love him, be connected with him, sharing profound intimacy with him. We have known tangible connection with God like Jesus, our relationship is based on spirituality the concept of conceiving truth, love, and prosperity are done on an intimate level of maturity which allows us to overlook that physical nature of relationship you see we are so caught up in touching feeling game it is so pathetic my brother to a point we don't allow our mental relationship to grow. Brother CA, we need to get to know who sister are love them respectfully, appreciate them entirely, talk to them candidly, and support them unconditionally you feel me my brother this is called MATURITY to its highest quality no matter your physical extremities maybe telling you lol cause it's NOT all about SEX all the time. Once we can grasp the true nature of intimacy towards our BLACK women our nation will become strong.*

QGB- King KS you said that! (Applauding)! I couldn't agree more with your statement in full...Smiling

KS- Thank you my beautiful queen, but we (man)must learn how to treat our Sista with respect therefore respect will be returned you remember back in the days listening to Marvin Gaye and the stylistic they song about love how a man should be towards a female all this rap shit is not the same when we had grandmaster flash, public enemy and KRS1 rapping about strength and power brings unity I loved ourselves, this New shit [excuse my tone] is bringing us down. Fuck this! Let me suck and lick this all sorts of male feminism toward our BLACK youth. Don't get me wrong, I love pleasing my Sista, but we have to regain consciousness again in order to find true love with one another, queen. Stay focused. Your brother KS.

CA- *I am sorry it took me so long to respond to this response; however, I have been busy all day; having said that, I think you should reread your response: You stated "intimacy" with an unseen person or object; you state our intimacy with God without having seen him, etc. and you mentioned Jesus!" You cannot have a relationship with anything you cannot see feel or touch, that's a scientific fact, and as far as God is concerned, who is God? You cannot tell me, I know that, so how can you have a relationship with something or someone you do not know; my Bible teaches me, "God is a Spirit," and the word Spirit means Mind, so if you had a relationship with God, who said I am the first and the last, and besides me, there is no other, you would not believe in a fake Jesus; your responding to my post, evidences that you cannot have a relationship with someone you don't know, are we in a Relationship? Reread your response and research this false teaching of Jesus, and all the lies Black Americans have been taught; nevertheless, I commend you for speaking your mind although you are misinformed, so I believe God has a great work for you; keep speaking your mind because it is in doing so that we find truth, be blessed!*

KS- *What is your Bible?*

WSC- THAT WOULD BE VERY HARD, I'M NOT SAYING IT CAN'T BE DONE! THIS ALSO DEPENDS ON WHAT TYPE OF RELATIONSHIP WE ARE TALKING ABOUT.

SS- *Yes u can have a long-distance relationship while some still be having relationship right were they at. They still be f**k.*

EBAS- *I Use to Have Faith in A Long-Distance Relationship. But I've Since Found Out It Doesn't Work. If You Are Dealing with A Person Who Has Never Been in A Faithful Relationship. In His Life. Love Hurts Sometimes but With God's Help. I Will Move on And Maybe Just maybe the Next Time It Will Be a Faithful and A True Love Relationship.*

ME- Yep but when you finally together it may not be so rosy. The challenge is always becoming one without totally losing you.

PG- No you are missing the whole relationship.

KING-ISMS

I have a confession to make, but I want you to keep it just between us, okay? I love the movie Love Actually — love it. Really, I do. I know that this is not the most masculine thing to admit, but I'm okay with that because I'm just a sucker for that movie. I don't even mind that Hugh Grant is in it. Although I am a big softie for all the varied (though mostly archetypal) story lines in that film, the one that I am most drawn to is the narrative between Jamie (the spurned lover/writer) and Aurelia (the beautiful Portuguese woman who takes care of the summer house where Jamie writes his murder mystery novel). The love that these two people share is so powerful that it transcends time, location, and even language; and (spoiler alert!) Jamie ultimately hops a last-minute flight to Portugal where he professes his love and proposes to Aurelia in front of the whole town on Christmas Eve, and they will presumably live happily ever after in either England or Portugal.

Among the many reasons that Jamie and Aurelia's relationship is pure fantasy (good fantasy mind you, but fantasy nonetheless) is that it is based on the idea that long-distance relationship can be magically transformed into the perfect domestic relationship that we all (well, at least people like me, who love movies like Love Actually) dream about.

In real life, long-distance relationships don't work. The reason that they don't work is that, like Jamie and Aurelia's relationship, they are a fantasy.

Long-distance relationships often masquerade as real relationships. They can be passionate, intense, and loving. But what they can't be is battle-tested. Developed romantic relationships require commitment, contact with reality, but most of all, they require action. Because most of the time spent together in long-distance relationships is precious, most problems are ignored. As a result, long-distance relationships usually exist in a suspended "honeymoon state," where everything is shiny and happy but devoid of the reality that is necessary to determine if the relationship will ultimately sink or swim. Therefore, many long-distance relationships fail. There are some exceptions to the rule. Let's consider these:

Relationships that are forced to become long-distance for a defined period (e.g., because of time-limited school, economic or military commitments) generally do not fall into the fantasy trap because they are very much based in the realities and practicalities of life. As a clinical psychologist, I have seen these types of relationships thrive. From my experience, successful long-distance relationships appear to have four factors in common:

1. **Prioritization**: When you consciously prioritize your long-distance partner above nearly all your local social commitments, you will be less likely to resent the effort required to make the relationship work.
2. **Commitment:** Commit to spending more than just weekends together. The more time you spend the greater, the chance to deepen the bonds between you and the more opportunity you must really get to know each other.
3. **Sharing:** If you are in a long-distance relationship, make sure that you don't just spend the time you have together alone. Share your social/family worlds with each other. We are all part of communities. When we cut our partners off from our communities they don't really get to know who we are.

4. **Planning:** If you are serious about the relationship begin planning for a time (soon) when the relationship will no longer be long-distance but when the two of you will be together in the same place. This will allow the relationship to have some forward movement so that it doesn't exist in a suspended state for too long.

If you are currently in a long-distance relationship or are considering getting into one, I strongly encourage you to consider how to apply these elements to your relationship. If you do, you and your love just might end up like Jamie and Aurelia — happily ever after (sigh).

Your Answer

CHAPTER 3

Your man had a hard, stressful day. What does he get when he gets home?

QUESTION: Your man had a hard, stressful day. What does he get when he gets home?

AY- I'd cook his favorite meal and put him in the tub. Play his favorite music and have candles burning. Give him a massage and oil him up and give him something relaxing. Hum mm. Lol!

SE- I'm running him a warm bath, having him a cold soda and a warm meal... Once he is done bathing and eating I'm rubbing him down in lotion and giving him a back and neck massage.

AGFL- Give him a drink of his choice...coffee tea or me lol a deep tissue massage from head to toe and Let him talk it out.

AOH- Oh trust!! He won't be stressed anymore!! Mama Queen got him good!!! What's known don't have to be spoken!!

CS- Okay back to reality nothing's going to happen either she been running around all day or she been working herself she gives you like 5 minutes to vent and then she's going to go take her shower and lay down and dinner well you should have pick up something on your way home LOL PS get your ass back on your side of the bed I'm tired.

DB- For some. Not all 😄☐

NKBSW- Almost what CS said. However, dinner would be done. I would ask if he's ready to eat. I would ask what happen. Take shower & ask if u need a massage. If he doesn't bit & I am not horny. I'm sleep or on chill mode.

TH- I take all his stress away with all his favorite things.... I mean all his favorite things.

CJW- Dinner, shower, back rub, prayer and off to bed! Listen if he's desiring to share the day with you. Without taking over the conversation or making it about you...

AND- Whatever he desires. SOOO fa real. Been there.

QGB- I then become his comforter helping him to prepare for a nice hot shower and body massage from head to toe. Make sure that his home cooked meal is warmed up as we eat dinner together. If he needs to vent give him silence and my ear. If he needs to just lye his head in my lap as he caresses my soft and sweet smiling skin, it's his for the asking, with no words necessary! If he wants us to just hold each other in silence, slipping into the act of making intense love, it would be his to have at whatever moment pleasures his whim! Whatever my baby wants, my baby gets; after God himself, I am and will be his comforter. I will then speak to the King in him, as I remind him to give it to God and walk away from it...Smiling

SLJ- Listen, without interruption. Comfort, which includes, but not limited to...Favorite meal, dessert, Beverage etc., Shower, comfy clothes...or whatever pleases, eases his mind...to lock out the troubles from work related stressors. If he needs to complete an assignment. I'm there too...We're in this together. If work is not due...phones re off...It's his time to unwind, chill and release. I got my Hun Bun!!!!!

GP- FANTASTIC ANSWER SANDY!!! Now just spread the word to the other women that doesn't know this prescription 4 a harmonious relationship. And the man should also do the same 4 his woman when she has days like this!! I believe they call it "Give and take!!"...😊☐ 😊☐

EAH- Make sure I do not add to his stress. #peaceathomeEqualJoy

DB- Ask him what HE NEEDS to erase all his stress of the day and proceed to accommodate his relaxation...I would make it all about him 🖤👊👍

MC- It's rated Xxtra special, I'll keep that to myself. 😊
RRSH- Peace he gets no noise. Hot dinner if he chooses to eat. Bubble bath, bathing beads. His favorite relaxation tracks. And anything he wants after a full warm oil body massage.

PG- Listen to him ... Hold him let him feel you there for him just listen.

RD- I would have his dinner cooked and have him a 🔥 bath waiting on him and let him tell me what else he wanted because he was the one that had a bad day.

DB- I have his favorite meal ready for him to eat run his bath light some candles give him a nice massage. And some good old loving.

SJ- Treat Him Like a King!
MB- Bath dinner conversation then Mr. nasty time!

EBAS- He Will Receive All My Attention Starting with A Big Hug 😊 Then A 💋 Kiss. Then I Would Draw Him A Steaming 😤 Hot Bath 🕯 Wash His Hair and Entire Body with Essential Lavender Oils. Gently Drying Him Off. Then I Would Give Him a Total Body Massage. Then What Ever Comes Next. Most Likely Some Charlie Wilson Then Some Sexual Healing from His Now Forgotten Stressed 😩 Day!!! Ijs

GP- Hmmmm!!!..😊

EBAS- How You Like Me Now King GP? I'm thinking that you have ONE LUCKY MAN!!! 👍 👍 👍..😊 😊

I Don't Have the Answers, But I Do Have Some Questions

EBAS- 😄

NM- Food if he hungry, drink if he thirsty, room or space if he need it, and a listening ear with a closed mouth if he needs to vent.

KING-ISMS

Anyone ever had to deal with a stressed-out man in your life? Well if you have, you know it sucks. As we know, men, as simple as they like to be, become really complicated when it comes to stress. And it can be so darn frustrating because that's where we feel we can be a "pro" at helping and talking through it! But chances are, if your man is stressed, he doesn't like to talk about it much. So, what's a girl to do?

First, we need to realize that men don't always stress out about the same things as women. Or if we are stressed about the same thing, we approach it differently than the man in our life would.

Secondly, take note of the signs of a stressed-out man. Chances are he's not going to come to you in tears wanting to talk about it. Is your husband (boyfriend, etc.) …

- Quiet… too quiet
- Starting to get "short" with you
- Never wanting to talk about work (or the thing you think might be stressing him)
- Getting set off by seemingly small things?

If you answered "yes" to any of the above, your husband could be stressed!

Be flexible about your lifestyle, be willing to make changes. Tell your husband that you are proud of him, but you care more about his happiness and your relationship than the money he brings in; let him know you'd be willing to make changes if it would mean a happier husband!

Be observant of your husband. Take notice if he's acting any of the ways I mentioned in my intro. If he is, watch out for when he opens to you. Many men will be ok with talking to you about what stresses them, in their own time. And when that happens, listen. Always be open and honest, but also choose joy. Make your home a happy place to come home to and let your man know you're happy to see him. Encourage your man to do something fun that maybe he hasn't done in a while! Keep in mind that it doesn't have to be without you! I'll bet you $10 bucks (ha, not really. That's like two Starbucks) that your guy would love to go out and do one of his favorite hobbies with you! Get him to having fun and laughing and let him forget about his stress, even just for a little while.

Ok ladies, I'm confident that if you follow some (or all these tips), that you will be doing everything in your power to lighten the burden of stress he carries and remind him that you love him, and it's going to be ok. That's not to say that what he's worrying about isn't real.

Men are usually pretty good at only worrying about the big stuff. But knowing that he's not alone and that all the pressure doesn't rest solely on him to fix it will be sure to bridge that gap of distance that stress can force into a relationship.

Your Answer

I Don't Have the Answers, But I Do Have Some Questions

CHAPTER 4

Men, the sex would be off the charts if she just stops......?

QUESTION: Men, the sex would be off the charts if she just stops…...?

JEB- Making Me Beg. Don't make me #Beg. ..😂

OC- Wow man just, wow!

MW- I have anything to say 5 min couldn't come up with nothing speechless. Lol

PA- A wise man once said nothing! He let her vent, then they had sex!

GP- TALKING!!!...Lol!!!

EBAS- How You Going to Know What We Want If We Don't Talk. 😊

GP- EBAS Not tooting my horn, But I can safely say that I've had NO COMPLAINTS!! If I'm into you and IT, talking is a distraction. Taking away the moment. Have this ever happened 2 U? It works both ways. IJS

EBAS- Yes It Has Ok 👌 Got King GP I Hear 👂 You Sir. lol My 👄 Lips 🤐Sealed 🤐

GP- Don't seal them now!!... LOL!!...😂 😂 😂

KS- If she quit complaining about my high sex drive.

IM- Amen!!

JR- If I just sit and don't say nothing?

I Don't Have the Answers, But I Do Have Some Questions

JR- Men God did not want us to talk or speak what we had to say. Never gave us a mouth. So, you give your lady 100% plus more. Their a door doesn't let it stop from walking.

LC- Holding back. Let loose girl. Go for what you want, need! The bedroom should be a no judgment zone.

SB- Holding back!

KS- Well help him release that stuff, a little bit of romance on the kinky side won't hurt anyone, you have to be the seductive smooth beast in bed in order for him to open up men love a challenge in bed I know I do lol lol.

EC- Yes, they do. Lol

JPR- Giving Directions.

JR- Just saying men and woman's always playing these games. Not giving 100% because he said she said. Just remember when your lady or man looking for it somewhere else can't get upset!

AP- He said KINGS. So, Y are QUEENS replying?

TP- Cause we crazy

EC- Now, by the answers forth given. KINGS! FOR THOSE OF YOU THAT WOULD LIKE FOR US TO STAY QUIET WHILE HAVING SEX TO MAKE IT BETTER. IT WILL NEVER HAPPEN. LOL ✌️👅❓😄⬜

DF- Nothing if I am doing what needs 2b done trust n believe she doing what needs 2b done

KING-ISMS

Do you want to know the real reason why men give up sex? It's not what you think.

So, you're in relationship with a guy, or you've been in a relationship with a man, and he stops giving you sex. Suddenly it just dries up and dies. (The sex, I mean). So, what does a woman usually do in this situation? Women usually do a couple of different things, and what they do is usually ridiculous.

Women create a story inside their head because they talk to their other women friends, and their other women friends will say that he must be cheating or must be having an affair. So now that seed is planted in a woman's brain.

So, what's the next thing she does? She'll start looking around the house for affair notes or anything she can. She becomes a CSI investigator. Oh, yeah! She's looking for affair fingerprints anywhere she can possibly find them. If she can, she'll grab his cell phone and go through all of his text messages and try to find something that's incriminating—even if it's a text message to one of his buddies. She'll dig through the phone book and see if there's any new people in there. Then she'll go for the e-mail. "Yeah! There's got to be something in that e-mail account that they have. Yeah! I'm going to find it". That's what Tiger Woods' wife did—she found an email. They'll look through and they'll just click on any e-mail from a woman. "There's got to be a woman in there somewhere. Got to find it". And what do they find? They always find an email to a woman, and then they create a story based on the email that they found. Oh, and the story she tells her friends afterwards is always great. "I found an e-mail to a woman. Yeah! You should see it. They were being nice to each other in there!" Because men and women can't be nice to each other unless there's a penis and a vagina involved, right?

What's crazy is the fact that these women go into CSI investigation mode while the answer to all their problems is right in the mirror.

The real reason why most men stop having sex with their girlfriends or their wives is because they're not emotionally connecting. That's right. We're emotional creatures too. We like to emotionally connect.
We need it, especially the men that are wired with more foreplay—emotional, mental, and physical—in mind.

It's never what you think. It really isn't. The last thing a guy in that situation is really thinking about is a fling. A fling? Yea, that's exactly what he wants: to bring another woman into his life and complicate things even more. Right?

So, the next time you suspect your man of cheating or having a fling, ask yourself, "What is my man really about? How does my man like to feel? Is my man an emotional guy?" Maybe he's just reaching out to other people, communicating with people, friends, family, whatever it might be, to try to figure out how to salvage the relationship.

We don't think with our penises ladies! all the time. We tend to also think with our hearts, and sometimes when our heart is broken, we don't want to repair it through physical attention from another woman. We want to repair it through conversation, through healing, through getting better.

The next time you suspect your man of cheating, consider that maybe he's a little deeper than you thought he was.

Your Answer

CHAPTER 5

Your mate confesses to cheating; do you need to know with who and why?

QUESTION: Your mate confesses to cheating; do you need to know with who and why?

DR- Deep!

SE- Nope but I do need him to quickly get his shit and tear his ass

AJS- I my self-need to know why. Especially if I treated her like a. Queen with the upmost respect and was loyal to her to. Yes, tell me. Why?

CG- Wow!

KS- No, it's over. Under no circumstances will I tolerate cheating or physical abuse.

DT- I don't need to know or why. Just get out and don't come back!! There's no need for anyone to cheat just leave if you don't want to be with he/she.

MW- Nope! There is no good reason for cheating. COMMUNICATION!!! If that's doesn't work walk away.

MJ- Neither because I have been cheated on and that shit hurt. He can pick up his things leave my key and keep it moving. Oh, yeah I will be changing the locks just in case.

KS- But what if you live with him lol Just trying to make you laugh but I do agree with what you said

MJ- Oh, shit I guess I must suck it up until I can move. Js
PW- I need to know "why?", unless it was with a friend or family member I don't need to see with whom, but a friend or family member I need to know "why?" from them as well.

I Don't Have the Answers, But I Do Have Some Questions

DR- That's smart.

FFF- Nope after he confess there is no need for nothing the only thing needed is for his behind to get up out of my face...Cause whatever the need was it clearly wasn't me 🙎‍♀️❓❓♀️❓➖❓😒⬜

QGB- It doesn't matter; it'll be time to move on for me!

JB-No I don't...I just want him gone...

AB- Nope, cheating is a choice you make... I'm gone!!

CM- BOTH...

RK- None of that it's simple, okay I'll Holla at cha....... if you really love someone your spirit will have told you before they did.

PL- No. I don't care. Just quickly get your stuff and go move in with her...

DR- KING-ISMS as always very THOUGHT PROVOKING!

GB- No, there is no requirement to know why and/or with whom. He can go his way because I'm out. ACTION IS ALWAYS LOUDER THAN WORDS.

KKD- It's enough information for me to say see ya around sometime.

DA- No spirit of forgiveness? Your mate told you. You didn't catch him/her. That's a place to start to mend a broken relationship. Maybe even make it stronger. Life is hard, and marriage is harder. People mess up. Just glad Jesus didn't dip on me every time I messed up. I certainly have the spirit of forgiveness **Queen DA**- I just don't have it in me to forget or trust him again. With the deceit there had to be lies as well. I truly believe that it would be in me one day down the line to somehow hurt him right back; and, expect forgiveness from him as well. I believe that this pain would regrettably take me there just from wondering what he's doing or where he's at, when things don't match up. I'd rather leave the situation instead of running myself crazy. Just my thought's Queen!

DA- Well Queen I guess we each must start with is the relationship worth saving. If it is that means forgive and forget. Takes real work. No tit for tat. No fair saying you're 15 minutes late where were you. I'm talking serious work here. Now if it's a serial deceiver like that female that slept with her son in laws and got pregnant - well must forgive her too for your own sanity but there's no forgetting that level of deception. Guess it depends on the situation. Much love Queen

AT- There was a time when I would have wanted to know both...at this age, all that matters is he disrespected me and our relationship #buhbye

MG- I know why hell he chooses to. No need to know who it won't change what's already done n I don't want any visuals renting space in my mind.

MC- Currently, cheating can alter your life or cost your life...no Bueno.

I Don't Have the Answers, But I Do Have Some Questions

BH- I would want to know the answers to those questions. Just because we are married does not mean I own him. If he made that decision I would expect for him to tell me all the details and from there we would decide as two adults where our relationship will go.

Do I condone him cheating? No. But I understand that I don't Own him and before we are anything, we are friends and as such we can talk about whatever.

RG- I can write a book on these cheating games. Can break up your home do stay or walk away. It LEAD to UNHAPPY days. For some UNHAPPY DAYS.

PA- Can't really say what one will do just would not want to be tested 🙏☐

NB- No why bother. That's a deal breaker. Bounce don't let the door hit u on your way out.

NC- I need to know with whom so she doesn't try to be up in my face smiling like nothing!

AL- People say they will be out in an instant, then why are there so many that stay?

QGB- Because they're not the one's who'd be out! Lol
JH- I would need to know why...in case there is something I need to change in myself. I need to know with whom, in case I know the other individual, so I can cut her too...I mean cut her off.

NG- I'm done don't give a fuck for real!

DB- Nope... Don't need to know nothing about why..who..what..when..I only need to know when you stepping 🖤☐🙏☐

CA- 99.9% of all women I have met in my lifetime had lost their virginity when we met; in other words, they had already had sex before meeting me; consequently, it was too late to save her virginity for me, so if I had a woman to tell me that, I would let her know that I appreciate her honesty, and I would not want to hear details as to why or with whom, but I might ask, what did it mean to you other than getting wet?

JW- Yes and yes... Exactly what KING-ISMS said because there are 3 sides to every story.

KPS- Only if it was a woman...then I would know definitively that there was nothing that I could have done. If it was a guy, I don't want to know who...maybe their justification on why.

KING-ISMS

I would want to know who and why. I need to evaluate the situation to see if I played a role in not keeping her happy and satisfied along with contempt.

Your Answer

CHAPTER 6

Is a Trans-Woman still a man?

QUESTION: Is a Trans-Woman still a man?

MW- Just don't know the answer, and I don't encounter them. What they call themselves to me is irrelevant to me.

VV- They are still human

QGB- No one is saying that they're less then human King VV; just wanting your opinion is all!

RK- In my opinion if you were born with a penis you're a man.

GAC- Agree...even if it's reconstructed to be something else!!!!

CCP- Agree

PSR- Wowzers lol, ijs

PB- They still think like a man!

QGB- If you were born a Man, there is no amount of surgery in the world that can convert that! Point Blank Period!!!

MW- I think you are thinking sexually. But people are born with the opposite personality. It's who they are in their mind.

QGB- I'm thinking humanly is what I'm thinking! Nothing more nothing less! You are the sex that God created you to be, there's no way around it!

KS- Preach Queen!

KT- Ummmmmm yes you are

AC- Genetics can't change identity can. I will identify with the person both their genetics.

TS- No matter how you look at it even though it's transformed it still has the mind of a man..

KT- You know there is so much more to being a woman than wearing dresses, being able to walk in heels or adding extensions, just because one look like a woman does not make them a woman.

MW- No, but a man can be mentally female scientific fact, as well as both sexual organs.

AJS- Whatever you were born. That's who you are regardless of what your decision may be later. One birth. Boy or girl.

MW- Not true. Babies born male can have female personalities, and have male bodies.

AJS- There is no worse way to insult a woman. Then she looks like a man. But once a woman gets over that there is. Words by. Wendy. Williams

MW- But you are looking at it from a nonscientific view point. Nature is different, it makes variants, we relate to each other according to our norms. But babies are born with different personalities, they can have male bodies and female Personalities. They can even have both male, and female sexual organs. Because of religion, and prurient norms we get excited by someone's outward appearance and sexuality. I chose to look the other way. I am a Christian, so I have a philosophy about sexuality, but in my real-world outlook I, have to except the people for who they portray themselves to be even if I don't accept it. You can say born boy equals boy, but now they can declare, but psychologically they could be female. Its open now and we think of things only in sexual terms, but some of these people, not all, were born that way.

MW- Some of you lady's sound threatened. IJS. They have their own world, so I doubt they care what others think. Some think of them as psychologically man, or female. If they do that much to be the opposite sex, I would think the opposite sex is who they feel like. It's should not be thought of in the sexual way, but it is.

NW- Ha Ha never that if anything you men need to be worried what you might pick up at the club thinking you got a chick when in fact it's a dude #dudelookslikealady

MW- I have never been fooled. I also don't pick up at the club. I was responding to another member post. A male and a female. But I also think men know the difference. I do.

LDD- The experts call it body dysmorphia.

QGB- I haven't seen not one post where someone sounds threatened MW, if anything I'm reading some that seems defensive for the characteristics of such beings! They may feel what they feel; yet, they simply are who they are, MEN! HMMMMMMM

MW- To you, but not them. We identify people physically, but we are more than physical self, we have minds. As far as my statement that was on some reactions like "point blank period"!!! Personally I try to respect a person's depiction of themselves and keep going. I don't try to understand. Not my job to.

QGB- That's you! My opinion belongs to me; so why are you trying to understand or depict what I feel.

MW- Oh sorry, I should have said ladies, and gentlemen.

QGB- No apologies necessary, just as I thought I'd be addressing a King and Queen!

MW- I was not depicting what you feel, I was interpreting the sentiment of what you wrote. And I was not apologizing, just acknowledging that I did not include the fellas who also had that impression.

KC?- Check please!

CKI- If they get the surgeries done they aren't

PL- A penis doesn't make a man nor a vagina a woman. CHROMOSOMES decide one's sex. You can cut it off, put it on, but if you were born a woman, you ARE still a woman, and vice versa. That isn't my opinion, just scientific fact.

SB- No matter how you feel inside or how many surgeries you have you will always be What God made you to be, Just my thoughts.

MW- From one's religious perspective, people have a mental personality.

SB- Still a man!

MW- Well won't change your mind, but I had a cousin who I grew up with he never crossed dressed as far as I know but he was mentally female to the day he died. In those days, we called them punks it was not just a sexual, he had a female
personality, that's who he was inside since I remember age5 maybe. I don't feel comfortable around
people like this, but it is a reality, especially now because of their civil rights. New world.

CG- I understand my cousin too, but he still a man!!!!! I'm comfort being around him my blood.

CK- Once you have had the surgery by law now their gender has changed.

SB- Law does not overcome what God.

CG- Still a man!

ADN- Long as a pole is settling in the center of their 🍑's. IT'S A MAN. ✔✔

DP- Right !😄😄😄😄😄

SB- Of course people can and will do what they want, I judge no one, I'm just voicing my thoughts.

QGB- We can certainly have an opinion without judging; it's called a discussion!

SB- Of course, I'm all about discussing things, but we all know discussions like this the first thing someone will say is who are you to judge

QGB- And they're judging with that comment! Lol Wow!

KW- Don't matter if you got the biggest breast, the biggest butt, the prettiest hair style, cutest face... if you came into this world with cock and balls you're a man. I don't care but this is how some people get mislead and that's when the shit hits the fan!!!!

ALT- Still a man but I will accept what he says and respect it.

NW- If you still have that penis...saying until you blue in the face doesn't negotiate that fact.

CA- From face value, the responses seem on target, if you will, but let's look at it, "If you came into this world with cock and balls you're a man!" Ok, based on that statement, we ask, "does a dog have cock and balls? the answer is yes, so we ask, is a dog a man? I think we all would agree that a dog is not a man; therefore, we have missed something because a man is being defined as cock and balls whereas there are many animals with cocks and balls, but they are not men; therefore, we cannot define a man as cock and balls; moreover, in Scripture we read: "When I was a child, I acted like, but when I became a man, I put my childish ways aside...." Therefore, we must conclude that genitalia have nothing to do with being a man because the writer in question obviously had cock and balls, but was not yet a man; in addition, the question, in a very real sense, is an oxymoron because it states: " Trans Women Are Not Men!" Therefore, we look at trans Wo--men are not men; nevertheless, hyphenated, we have an adjective describing a kind of men, wo--men; consequently, we're simply describing another kind of man, and considering all the facts, we must conclude that man is defined as a state of mind relative to a gender but not a gender because Scripture teaches us, "God created both wo-man and man, so what we have here two kinds of men; a wo-man and a man, so I conclude that both wo-man and man are states of mind or consciousness!

LPR- God created you as a man no matter what you change about yourself to become a woman your genetic makeup is that of a male you are male regardless if you call yourself a female!

MW- People are all the time with female personalities, I am kind of shocked that people don't know it. Psychologist have known this since the 19th century.

EDD- Not my scene, none of my business.

KH- Transgender is still a man!! If u have a Penis you are a Man!!!!!

TRW- WTF a he-she man!

SEM- If you weren't born with ovaries and tubes. You're a man.

KP- It's a he, and he still bad he doesn't mind what he is he let people know but they still be trying it because his that bad.

EE- PANDORA'S BOX.... is real be careful!

CCG- If you're born a man you will always be a man, regardless of what changes you make to your body, and when you die, you will die as a man no matter what society says. That being said, if that is your thing, so be it.... but you're still a MAN!

TB- I always wonder about the tongue or the roof of the mouth, or just things that can't be changed like the bottom of your feet, how can that go from male to female I wonder.

CW- If they still have man parts they are just men with breast and hormone replacement.

CS- The hell they not y'all better quit holding Satan's hand too tight you might get burned!

BC- You are a DEVIL DEMON living inside of man MOCKING the very thing that GOD loves WOMAN.

I Don't Have the Answers, But I Do Have Some Questions

SH- So are you saying God makes mistakes? I don't agree. Humans make mistakes trying to change what the potter set forth because of a feeling, because their mind set, because our thoughts are not his thoughts and our ways are not his ways-- because we can't see the big picture to the mosaic picture !!GOD'S WAY IS THE TRUTH..AND THE TRUTH CAN STAND ON ITS OWN. THIS TO ME IS TRICKERY- DECEPTION BY WAY OF ILLUSION. LIKE A MAGICIAN ALSO PLAUSIBLE..LOOKS LIKE IT COULD BE REAL, BUT IS NOT. BUT TO EACH ITS OWN. EVERYBODY PAYS FOR HIS/HER OWN CHOICES. GOOD OR BAD. RIGHT OR WRONG..IJS...

BC- Go to Hell! People just Make up shit Just to live a Filthy Life! God made you a Man and MAN MADE You A WOMAN!! Get it STRAIGHT don't get it twisted RETARDED FREAK!!!

SH- You do know we said the same thing in own words. Right preacher God Bless you

JH- And water is not wet! And a pig with makeup on is no longer a pig!

BC- 🌊 water is wet and a 🐷 with makeup 💄 is still a pig because God is a PERFECT GOD and he created you as a MAN and you decided that YOU would like to be a WOMAN but your DUMB ASS is still what GOD created you to be and that is a MAN!!!

DH- What are they then????

MG- I believe it's deceptive. If you are born male, then that's what you are. They can't function as a female to have the option to procreate or even in my opinion have the mentality of a woman.

DM- Not real women either, they don't bleed nor do they give birth, not against them, just my opinion.

CF- If you weren't born with female parts the you're a man.

TBO- God made them Men So They are a Man no matter what They do to themselves!

MJ- Yes, they are men and they need mental health counseling. They are born as males, it does not matter what their mind says, They Are Men. The bitch is pretty.

MP- Be whoever you want to be!! I'm not the judge or jury of anyone!

TE- So what if they are born with both sexual organs? Then is it their choice on which gender they choose or what? How do you decide based on religion in that situation? And I'm not trying to contradict anyone's beliefs or opinions I'm simply asking out of curiosity.

QGB- I've always wondered the same thing Queen.

BN- People born with both sex organs are hermaphrodites. That is different since they are born with both. The don't decide to select on sex their parents do when they are babies. That must be a difficult decision to make. If those children change what their parents selected they are not trans in my opinion because they were born with both sex organs.

TE- Thanks!

QGB- Yes, with the parents deciding their baby's sex, they could feel differently growing into themselves the opposite of what was chosen! Wow!

BN- that must be a hard choice for a parent. They won't know until years later if they made the right choice or not. That poor child suffers.

QGB- I agree Queen!

TE- Yes ma'am I can't even imagine how much emotional anguish they will encounter and must endure. We always wonder as parents if we have our children's best interest at heart. But that's a tough spot for anyone.

QGB- So very true sweetheart, and we'll never know until they become adults. We must pray to God before making life altering decisions when it comes to their wellbeing! I'm sure this is one of the most difficult for sure...Wow!

TB- So do they replace the eye balls or is he still looking at me.......lol it's like putting lipstick on a pig.

TE- They still have all the strengths and everything God gave man within.... Regardless they're still a man no matter how womanly they look!

DB- Mentally no, in their minds they are women.... Physically they are men no matter the removal of the bat and balls...I respect which ever gender they feel they are. My opinion ♥☐👑☐

TFH- God made men and women not transgenders. God doesn't make mistakes. We do! It's a billion-dollar industry making butt implants, breast implants, tummy tucks, lips that look crazy, don't get me wrong, I am all for any woman who wants to improve with certain body parts and men too. But breast on a man and butt implants just looks crazy. I can spot them 10 miles away

DP- If they were born with a penis I beg to differ.

NA- This is my friend, and I love her, she is very beautiful. I wish people would let the GLBT live their lives. They are human and wish to live their lives just like anyone else. I'm sure she is happy, you have one life to live, live it the way you see fit and do what makes you happy.

MG- Only she must answer for herself on judgment day not us.

KC?- But you just said she....Hummmmmm?

TB- Robbing banks makes me happy, and yet It's something I s shouldn't be doing.

NA- That has nothing to do with the issue at hand. I meant Gender wise. Feel free to be who you want to, to please yourself.

TB- Your response was to this and I quote; You have one life to live, live it the way you see fit and do what makes you happy. I apologize for the misunderstanding.

MC- Hi. My name is MC. I'm trans-animal. I was born a woman, but deep down inside, I'm really a polar bear.

TB- Be sure to get that operation. Polar bears have three nuts....lol

BN- We cannot change our anatomy. We can change otter appearance. We can do hormone therapy. We cannot place ovaries and cervix inside a transgender. So, a male that transforms their outer appearance is a transgender female, not female. This is my opinion and I do not condone violence against transgender people.

RH- This issue is getting drawn too thin. We are born what we are PERIOD. If a person decides to change from that it's their right and choice. No one is denying that, but it's a choice.

PW- No Transgender children are born with both sexes and are assigned the sex of male. They could be female instead of male, but that is what they are assign instead of waiting until they get older and check hormone levels too see what sex they really are. Now trans who are born male and wants to be a woman because they feel they are born in the wrong body I'm confused about that, but I don't judge!

SH- I feel they are lost to. Reprobate mind (insane)

PW-Transgender: noting or relating to a person whose gender identity does not correspond to that person's biological sex assigned at birth: the transgender movement; transgender rights.

EE- Some of y'all go way too far with the judgmental stuff when it's supposedly NOT UP TO US TO JUDGE! and then some of the same ones that pass judgement and condemnation on others based on religious beliefs, will themselves or have themselves dabbled in same sex activities and relationships. Most of the judgmental comments in this debate are from females many of which who may have had lesbian's relationships in their pasts. So, what made it okay or any different to get down with another woman and you two took turns strapping on a huge dildo to pleasure each other? Better yet, do you judge yourselves when you pleasure yourselves with foreign objects inserted inside of you to substitute what a man can do? I say all that to say again...BE CAREFUL OF PANDORA'S BOX, it's a slippery slope! (I personally know of super judgmental women that changed their tunes when the transgendered woman dropped a log from between their legs and then that same judgmental woman tuned into a thirsty thot!) 😁☐ 😁☐ REAL TALK.... If they don't impose themselves on any one else straight or otherwise WHY DO WE EVEN CARE WHAT ANYONE ELSE IDENTIFIES THEMSELVES

AS...? Give them MF their own bathrooms and just keep it moving! lol

TE- Well now! 😂🗆😂🗆😂🗆 tell us how you really feel 😄🗆

EE- Nothing against the Trans community whatsoever.

TE- Oh I'm sorry I should have phrased that better I was totally agreeing with you! 😄🗆

EE- I just wanted to make that clear that's all lol.

EE- There is NO SUCH THING as TRANSGENDER anyway if you choose to keep your anatomical parts it's called IMPERSONATION!! all that PRE-OP mess is BULLSHIT, if you're a fine ass "woman" with a big ass and big tits but drop a dick with balls from between your legs YOUR ASS IS A FEMALE IMPERSONATOR/IMPOSTOR! and that isn't being judgmental it is what it is. just like a woman that has wrapped down her tits, taken testosterone hormones and wears a strap-on she is a MALE IMPERSONATOR/IMPOSTOR simple as that!

PW-Ok where you been research it not Transvectors. Transgender there is a such thing!

EE- Pat, I'm not dumb baby, I know there is a word called Transgender as this is an umbrella that those that feel like nature played an awful trick on them so they seek to identify with the opposite gender than they were born into but it's just a word identifier especially for those that go as far as to look the part that they want to be as well as acting it out but then fall short of going through with gender reassignment. In the case of so called "she male" transgender women...why call yourself transgender or she male when you are attracted to dudes and keep your anatomical male reproductive parts knowing you want to stick another guy in his ass or be stuck? Isn't that called being gay?

QGB- You'd better say that King EE. They're always trying to make things sound cute; example being "Transgender"! When indeed it is someone impersonating someone else! This makes too much sense to me...Wow!

PW- Eric Evans no you still missing the point they are not gay or lesbian. I see this different from you. The male is not the problem they are male and like women. It's the women who at birth are labeled men when they were really born a female. Just have a penis and a vagina. I called you dumb wouldn't do that respect my black man!

PW- QGB it makes sense if that is what is happening. Females are assign as a male at birth because of the penis when they are really girls. Just research it and you will understand it better!

PW- Let me make myself clear not man who wants to be a woman, but a baby that has both sexes are assigned as a boy when they are girls.

QGB- If you're speaking of hermaphrodites I understand that Queen PW. Allowing parents to pick the sex of their child whose born with both sexes! That I have no understanding about as far as the scientific part of it; but I feel for the child who chooses the opposite of what their parents decided for them. I see that as different if you were born male and you decide you wanna be a woman and consider yourself as such fraudulently! Everyone have their own life to live and deal with; yet, not keeping it real with the men that they meet until during or after a sexual encounter is Wrong! Do you, while not deceiving other's doing so!

PW- But they are still compared to gays and lesbian.

QGB- Ikr! It's sad and must be damn near impossible to deal with the different stereotypes that they're being labeled as! I really believe when they become interested in someone, they should immediately discuss their plight in life, and allow the person to make-up their own minds about it. No, everybody doesn't need to know their personal business; yet, for someone they look to become intimate with, shouldn't be kept in the dark. Not everyone will see them in the arena of being a freak of sorts. Whether they're turned down or not; they are being real and respected for it!

PW-Transgender: noting or relating to a person whose gender identity does not correspond to that person's biological sex assigned at birth: the transgender movement; transgender rights. You see that assigned at birth. If you are born a girl or a boy, you don't have to be assign because your identity is already known!

WSC- THIS IS MY OPINION, IF YOU HAVE MALE SEX ORGANS, YOU ARE A MALE, IF YOU DON'T HAVE PERIODS, IF YOU HAVE SPERMS, YOU ARE A MALE, IF YOU CAN'T CARRY A BABY FOR 9 MONTHS YOU ARE A MALE! I WON'T GO ALONG TO GET ALONG! CALL YOURSELF WHAT EVER YOU WANT TO, YOU WILL HAVE TO ANSWER TO GOD! I'M NOT MAD AT YOU, WE ALL FALL SHORT OF THE GLORY AND FOR ALL MY SINS WHAT EVER THEY MAY BE, I MUST ANSWER TO GOD! I BELIEVE THIS, GOD MADE MAN AND CREATE WOMAN FROM HIM TO BE HIS MATE TO EPRODUCE! JUST AS VALET AS YOURS. WHEN MAN INTERFERES WITH GOD'S CREATIONS, THEY WILL HAVE TO ANSWER TO GOD! NO MATTER WHAT ALTERATION YOU HAVE, YOU WILL HAVE TO ANSWER TO GOD!!! NOT TO GET THINGS TWISTED, THERE ARE PEOPLE THAT ARE HERMAPHRODITE FOR AND IN-BETWEEN. A HERMAPHRODITE ARE BORN WITH BOTH ORGANS AND TRANSGENDER ARE BORN OF ONE SEX AND DESIRE TO BE OF THE OTHER SEX AND I STATED GOD IS IN CONTROL AND HIS WILL, WILL BE DONE!!!

I Don't Have the Answers, But I Do Have Some Questions

NM- I'm sorry but yes, they are. They also need to be honest with these men in the beginning. What you choose to do with your life and sexuality should not be forced on anyone. Give them the disclosure up front.

JP- But they should be honest with the men they date.

QGB- Absolutely they should!

PG- Oh yes, they are!!! Do they have uterus's no!

SK- WHAT THAT BIRTH CERTIFICATE SAY?

EE- To be totally honest, I'm of the belief now that people that use the word TRANSGENDER use it as a crutch or tool to deceive or profit from. Why do I say that, because there are those that call themselves models and escorts that make big money exploiting the niche curiosities of men and women with eccentric /eclectic sexual tastes, desires, and preferences/perversions? Otherwise they'd completely gender reassign themselves quick fast and in a hurry. There's always a motive for them holding back on that last operation.

EH- They are to men, they still have a Dick!!!!

PG- Their something else man made doesn't make you a woman tranny, but you do you 🙄

RT- Then what are you?

SS- JUST men With Titties LMAO still love y'all

BM- The fact that this is even debatable is crazy.

TB- I'm old school and it's called Drag Queen, like instead of used its pre-owned, so instead of drag queen its now transgender. Lip stick on a pig will not make it stake.

KS- Sorry Queen and Kings. I just couldn't resist. Lolol. They men! God made you want he wanted you to be. Changing your body parts don't change the fact!

MW- Dam right!

LW-No they are not women.... I believe it could be a hormone imbalance that makes them feel they are. I don't understand why they don't try

taking hormones to help them feel like the gender they ARE instead of trying to become something they're NOT.

KS- That's a good point!

AB- Right like beef up the testosterone, don't sissify yourself. WTH!!! But hey the perverted is in!!! For those who accept it I certainly don't What God putting your crotch is what you are baby no chaser!!!

MW- Hello Queen Angel long time...lol Queen how are you sista

SB- If you don't have a uterus, you are a man with nice bundles. You can create a. Vagina, sir you are still a man.

GP- Why Are They Not??!! They were before they decided that they no longer wanted to be the sex that they were originally born/assigned to anymore. Nothing more to say!!!

MC- The big brow bone always gives it away for me...idc what their shape, makeup clothing...you can't cover it.

ABBT- Scrolling!

AB- Sometimes I think they don't realize the gravity of what they really are trying to be they want to be a woman with no. No uterus and can't have kids the whole point of you being a woman is that you do have a uterus you can get pregnant you do have a period. And you can't have children!! God made you a male for a reason you can reassign change and fake up whatever you please you are still a man and on Judgement Day you will be judged as a man the thing that makes me so upset is these so-called she males could beat the crap out of a woman because they are physically strong just like men because they still are men some of them can bench press 250 with the greatness of ease but want titties and a perky butt to taunt men with and pretend to be a female I wish they were female so that they can have the most horrendous menstrual cramps in the world I wish they were female, so they can endure childbearing and the pain thereof and all that comes after stretch marks included, but without but without any of these you are a man, a man who has cut off his penis so you can fake the funk and pretend to be something that you are not. it's almost an insult to the lowest degree that a man could ever even think to want to be something that God has purposed Us by Design to have by Nature the idiom of the people who are filled with the spirit of perversion who think that they will not be judged and people who are saying oh you're being judge. baby you are judged Everyday by the life you live whether you're a dirty crook a hooker a pimp those are all names of judgement and transgender means you're a confused individual who needs to spiritual Deliverance immediately I don't care if you don't like my opinion you got yours I got mine I mean this is the stupidity of the world think about it if everyone was homosexual in 20 years we be extinct as a people the whole purpose of your gender is procreation it is a design by God it's almost denial of God to deny who you really are. Point Blank I don't care who don't like it don't comment! and you are a twisted Wicked individual who wants people to agree and make laws to backhand God and stand behind your phony commitment to be something that God did not determine for you to be it is unnatural it is ungodly it is a twisted perverted mind that is trying to escape its own reality that would accept such a thing.

QGB- You just said that with conviction Queen! You speak the utter truth...Bammmmm!

AB- another thing another thing that irks my freaking nerve is people talking about oh you are judging oh you judging you're not supposed to be a judge if you're a Christian you need to go get your Bible there is a book in the Bible called Judges and what do you think they did!? it can also be found in the book of Isaiah that if I see my brother and sinning a sin not unto death and I convert such a one that the glory of God has risen upon me because I have hid a multitude of sins/faults but woe be unto me if I speak not the truth in the presence of my brethren I will not indulge and embolden a wicked conscience to go forward with any type of sin so they can call it judgement all day but if you asking for the truth here it goes I'm supposed to tell you when you're out of line and in Era as a child of God I'm supposed to warn you of the impending doom to come for the mistakes that you are making warning comes before destruction who do you think is the person that God is going to send to warn you it's going to be an individual with a mouth and you may call it judgement all day you're in error not knowing the word of God Jesus was the only one who did not condemn a man because he understood that you had a choice while you let yet live, but once you die in your Sin you will face not just the Judgment of our wagging tongues you will face the Judgment of Hellfire for being perverted please see First Corinthians 6:9 it says be not deceived God is Not mocked neither fornicators idolater's homosexuals or sodomites will enter the kingdom of God. I will roll a die first before I ever deny speaking to him the truth out of my mouth and what I'm speaking is the truth whether you like it or not whether it's politically correct or not have homosexuals in my family I have homosexuals in my community my daughter had a roommate who was a homosexual don't think that I spared the rod with any of them if you ask me a question like this expect the truth and if you can't say ouch then please a man, but get over because baby refuting it all day, that is never going to stop it from being the truth.

EH- You better bring it Sista!

WSC- YOU SPOKE THE TRUTH< IT DOESN'T MATTER WHO GETS UPSET, YOU HAVE YOUR RIGHTS ALSO! WHAT ALSO GETS ME THESE MALES COMPLETE IN SPORTS WITH FEMALES ALTHOUGH THEIR STRENGTH IS THAT OF A MAN, THAT'S WRONG! THEN THEY TAKE THE HONOR THAT RIGHTFULLY BELONGS TO A REAL FEMALE THAT WORKED SO HARD TO GET WHERE SHE IS AND THE LIST GOES ON!!!

VB- It takes more than an operation, reconstruction surgery and a hella weave job to fit the ranks of a woman and certainly a lady.

AB- oh come by here dear Lord say it again sister!

SN- OOH AMEN GOD MAKES NO MISTAKES. YOU WILL FACE HIM ON JUDGEMENT DAY. SO UNTIL THEN...PRAY.

EE- Hormone imbalance my ass it's called A GENERATIONAL CURSE!

RJC- ....of all of the no-business-being-news-shit, I have ever seen, this is the worst! Be who you were, at birth! THE ALMIGHTY, don't take kindly, to messing with HIS WILL! 😡☐

ID- To me it's still a man trying to crossover, but born a man, still a man.

RG- Yes u watch Jerry Springer. Ok.

KING-ISMS

Respect the words people use to describe themselves. Transgender people use many different terms to describe their experiences, and not all terms fit all people. It's important to ask people what language they want you to use. It's okay to ask someone for their preferred name and pronouns. Always use the name and pronouns they tell you.

If trans people aren't sure which identity labels fit them best, give them the time to figure it out for themselves. The terms or language a person prefers may change over time, and that's totally normal. That's okay. A person whose sex assignment at birth was male but whose gender identity is female. These identities can also refer to someone who was surgically assigned male at birth, in the case of intersex people, but whose gender identity is female. Many trans women identify simply as women.

Your Answer

CHAPTER 7

Can you be married and still lonely?

QUESTION: Can you be married and still lonely?

SE- Yes, being ignored, not being satisfied, not being made to feel of importance to the mate.

GB- If they don't love unconditionally. It won't work.

JPR- Yeah! When after you realize that things are not the way you expected.

SJ- Been There Done That LMAO I can do Bad by Myself!

EBAS- Absolutely. You Can Lose Interest in Your Mate. Lord Forbid Sickness Where Your Mate Checks Out Mentally and Physically. Such as Alzheimer's.

RK- You could be in a marriage for the convenience of it and not really be into that person, or maybe you've Grown Apart.

CD- By getting married for the wrong reason. Being married to someone who's not truly ready for real commitment. And the list goes on.

GGG- YES! YES! and YES!

PL- Yes. Loneliness has little to do with having another person present. It has everything to do with the quality of that relationship. That loneliness often causes people to stray, out of desperation for human contact...

DB- Yes. One can have a body near, but that person's mind may not be present which can cause the person to feel a sense of loneliness due to the fact of no presence of mind, only body ♥️ 🤜

VV- Very much so that's where on the other question of the day was would you date your neighbor? Haha!

NGN- Yes. Being Married encompasses many facets. Being in the presence of a man or woman every day doesn't mean you are interacting verbally or physically. And, if things aren't going well, the emotional detachment will make you feel alone even if the other aspects are present.

JEB- That's one of the main reasons for #Divorces is one of the parties starts to feel like they're #Lonely and not getting enough #Attention. Let Me Find Out...Until they leave and find out how really #Lonely that they are by themselves. . LMFAO.

PL-Most folks when they leave it's because they already have someone else.

JEB- PL, women do that...most Men if we make up our mind to leave. For me it doesn't matter if I somebody else or not... Um outta There (LMAO)

BR- If you are not sharing your emotional self or feel that you can. You feel put aside. And thus, lonely and alone even.

DGA- No communication.

MH- Yes when people grow apart.

CA- Loneliness is experiencing a void in our lives whether we are married or unmarried, and from childhood, my father being a preacher, I can still hear him singing, "My soul just couldn't be contented until I found the Lord!" I can say the same for myself and believe that no man cannot be lonely unless he has found the Lord; in fact, our purpose in life is to find God, and until we find God, though we may be married, we will this void or loneliness because it's the knowledge of knowing that regardless to whether we are in the company of thousands or alone. God is always with us because, as Scripture teaches, "For n him we live and move and have our being....," Acts 17:28.

LH- I WAS FOR 11 YEARS!

CD- I know, right? 19 yrs.

BH- Most of them lonely then single people just a piece of paper for the most of them. Always in someone else's business the ones I know.

TJ- YEP... been there done that!

KB- Painfully agreeable...since some people get married but have no commitment to the relationship with each other in their marriage, and most times it'll fail!!!

LH- Yes, I was married and a single parent and single.

ML- Yes, grab your purse and go!!!!

MG- I don't know about lonely but alone yes.

KI- Different words, but basically, the same meaning.

MK- Yes. If your spouse is physically present, has no desire to be adventurous inside and outside the house, or is stuck in a routine that bores you to death, you will be lonely.

SS- Yes if you're not doing any of the things with your spouse you have been planning for years to do, he's out doing him.

PW-Yes, if your spouse isn't emotionally presence.

GP- Yes, if married to the wrong person ijs.

EDLS- a title is not synonymous with emotion.

CC- Yes! So, frightening being linked to someone you have nothing in common with spiritually, physically or mentally!

ID- Scary but true

PP- Yes if you are not spending time with each other you will be lonely.

CA- Question answered, let's go to the next one!

KING-ISMS

If there's one thing worse than a miserable, lonely single person, it's a miserable, lonely married person. The irony is that no husband or wife marries with the intention of being isolated from their spouse. Most people believe that marriage is the cure for loneliness, but I want to warn you: You begin battling the dreaded foe of isolation as soon as you drive off on your honeymoon. Isolation has reached epidemic proportions in the most intimate of human relationships. In addition to more than a million legal divorces each year, isolation saps the strength from millions of marriages that still appear intact.

Your Answer

CHAPTER 8

Do all men pay for sex one way or another?

QUESTION: Do all men pay for sex one way or another?

JEB- Yes, we do QGB. My Daddy told me a long time ago. "Son...to be with a Woman, it's going to cost you Something. So, if she hungry go ahead and take her out to eat. Let Me Find Out... 🏆☐

NTN- Yen, when he bought that drink or put gas in his car to see you or purchased that box of condoms. Yes, one way or another without putting money in her hand. He paid.

SE- I believe they do, but it works both ways woman pays too.

MC- Yes, they do? But they front like they don't?

KI- Yes indeed, Hair/Nails done. Those dinners before WE pay!

JG- It's not just about sex, being what he's paying for!!

KI- It really isn't, but, at the end of the day, WE(should) want our Queen to represent the King that we are.

JG- YES King Kevin, you're right about that!!
And we, (Queens), should get to know and understand our Kings so that we can be the best Queen for them!

CG- Nope, The Things I Pay For, It's Out the Goodness & Kindness of My Heart... Peep Game: If you're doing it just for the sex, then what that makes her & You? Real Talk😎

JEB- CB you're all off basis Son. The moral of the story is simple. For a Man to be with a Woman in any capacity. Girlfriend, Date, Wife, Woman...It's going to cost him #Something. It doesn't work any other way. Let Me Find Out...

CB- So when she does things for you What Is It? Or You Can Be Bought? So, how's that for being way off. It is what It Is. What ever happen to just be kind & considering.

ME- And the one you claim not to pay for is the one you pay the most... ijs

JEB- CB Get your Mind Right Son. The question doesn't have anything to do with what she does or doesn't do. It Simply ask. do all Men Pay for Sex in One Way or Another. That's it and that's All Man! And the Answer to The Question is. YES! Bet you don't get that much.... LMFAO.😋❓...Let Me Find Out...U Talk to F'n Much!

JMS- So do women.

CB- You're on my comments with B.S. Grow The F!@k Up Fool. I must be right Because I Struck a Nerve. Oh, to correct you once again it is an act of if a person pays or does not pay. So, it does have a response if he or she pays. It's Called Action Words Idiot.

CA- I think we all can accept "One way or the other" because, as a man, if I do not have money on me or in my bank, I do not want sex, and the more money I have, the greater the sex; hey, I know that's not everybody, but that's me, not having any money is being sick, so how can I focus on sex when I am sick?

MW- Yes, Directly or Indirectly.

JEB- CB, I must have struck a #Nerve also got u cussing and fussing most of all. I got u explaining yourself. lmao. QGB sometimes these questions of the day. Just gets us all of Revved up n Riled. Keep it going. great question! I got #CBontheedge Bawahaha Lol.Let Me Find Out... 🏆□

I Don't Have the Answers, But I Do Have Some Questions

CB- Real Talk You came to me with your response to what I posted. Now it's your choice to comment neg. or pos. But to degrade me, that's another story. All in all, everyone has the right to express themselves freely. Real Talk.

QGB- You're somewhat in bully form my friend King JEB not necessary to get point across. Better addressed King to King! Respectfully.

JEB- As I've stated before I don't or didn't come from a docile world. And if King to King is left to work things out between themselves. Things will work themselves out. They usually do.

Let Me Find Out. What appears to women and sensitive men as #Bullying. is just Boys being Boys to me.

QGB- This Queen will stay in her place...Smiling

CB- Thank You Queen B Great Subject.

TW- Damn right and the joy is being able to have it to spend amen!

DE- 99.9% absolutely!

MC- Pimp/hoe, husband/wife, employer/employee. ..it's nothing more than an agreement. . someone is getting broken off either way you look at it.

JEC- Bawahaha LOL

MC- Am I lying?

JEB- Nah u Good MC, U not #Sensitive either. . u get a dozen 🌹🗆🌹🗆🌹🗆🌹🗆🌹🗆🌹🗆🌹🗆🌹🗆🌹🗆🌹🗆...from me. Let Me Find Out...LOL

BC- Yes, we do. Even if we brought them bubble gum we still paid for it. It's just that it was cheap.

RH- Yes, time and funds provided as the investment to the relationship.

VA- Everything has come with a price including our Salvation. Whereas we did not pay the price Christ did!

DM- Well you know what the saying is: Nothing in this world is free, not even conversation or bubble gum.

BT- Yes, I don't care if u bought hear a bottled water and chips. It is what it is.

VV- Yes, I'm sorry I have to say yes.

SH- Sure, but women pay for the D too.

MJ- Hell yeah! There's no way we're not.

CW- Yup P....sy Is the MOST EXPENSIVE ITEM ON THE PLANET....the curse of it.

SW- Yes even if it's your BF or Hubby.

BW- No, not All men pay for sex. If fact, some men have wealth or position and women throw themselves at them. Some men dress well, and have a nice car and women throw themselves at them. There are gentlemen who have little. In fact, they talk weak women into giving sex, money, car, and self-wealth.

DB- No... We do for one another financially...sharing is caring 🩶

TC- Nothing in life is free, especially not me" at least that's what the song says.

ID- Yes, they do wealth it be, conversation, dinner, movies, clothes, rent, car, etc. They paid.

KW- If you don't pay for it directly you'll pay for it indirectly as in anything that's leading to it for example gas to get there, hotel fees, eating, drinking!!!!

LW- No....there are cases where people are just "friends with benefits"....no dating involved.

EBAS- Not My Man His Benefits Are Renewed Daily. And His Benefits Comes as A Package Deal Neatly Packed by God.

GLS- Ladies Pay for it Too, Just Not as WIDE SPREAD & Talked about....

KING-ISMS

Single men pay for sex by picking up the tab while dating. Men and women date for many reasons, including companionship, not just sex. Many heterosexual couples share dating and travel expenses, and in many instances where gender imbalance persists, we must again look to larger issues of gender inequality.

All men want objectified sex. Just because some men, including some married men, engage prostitutes in what can only be considered objectified acts (as indicated by a list of "acts" with prices), it doesn't mean that many men aren't interested in better sex.

As anyone in a good relationship knows, sex can be both intimate and hot. These are not mutually exclusive categories. People need to break free from stale script and be playful with one another — this kind of behavior helps ensure both women and men are getting what they want sexually. Typically, women do want to have sex with their partners, but only if it is good sex.

I Don't Have the Answers, But I Do Have Some Questions

Your Answer

CHAPTER 9

Just Married! He's 19, and she's 44. Is age just a number?

I Don't Have the Answers, But I Do Have Some Questions

QUESTION: Just Married! He's 19, and she's 44. Is age just a number?

KG- Uhh in this case yeah. He's a baby and has nothing to offer but the obvious. Maybe he has a large inheritance and can take care of her.

TTA- It will be when he 50 and she 75! Lol

SJ- Nurp child Molester LMAO

ND- Not marriage material for me maybe something else!

BM- To a pedophile maybe lol.

LS- If they are truly in love, who am I to say no.... So, in this case yes age is just a number.

VQ- It won't last!!

MW- His life is just beginning, she more of a mother figure to him. I guess to each its own. But men have been doing this since the beginning of time and still is. This is a bit much.

CKI- Way too large of an age gap.

WSC- Old school, in my case I wanted someone I could grow old with, not someone already there! This is a bit much, he's probably just leaving the mother's nest, just to get another Mother! My opinion, let him make it, give him a chance to find out who he is, from her pose, the only message I'm getting, is sexual, lust, and it takes more than that for a marriage! Just my opinion! To each his or her own!!!

RDA- Age does not automatically give you matureness. I know 21-year-old men more mature than 40-year-old men. It all depends on the people involved. At a glance, yes, the gap is huge and questionable. But really without more info we are just judging the book by its cover instead of its content.

TH- All the mistakes she made and lived with the consequences of she is going to have to live with the consequences all over again as he makes the same mistakes as she did. The very same mistakes we all must make to grow into who we are. This will cause resentment in her then fighting then resentment in him. Way too much of an age gap.

SH- Don't judge the book by its cover until you've read the pages. But they look good together.

CT- Cradle robber....

JD- Yes until you realize that you are too many numbers apart. Because he hasn't experienced enough to communicate appropriately.

PL- That's not something I would want. It's his lack of life experience and maturity. Physically he would be in the prime of life, and that would be adventurous, but still a baby emotionally...no thanks!

CA- Yes!!!! If they both love one another then who is to judge them!!!! Mind My own business and be happy for them whatever age to couple is!!! Now that's my perspective.

TP- God bless you. Cause that man going to want a child trust me and he pray it's a boy to keep the cycle going

MBBP- Go head and preach Tammie.

TP- Thanks king

JJ- Why went a woman date or marry a man a lot younger than her she b label with all types of names when a man does it. everybody. Brags about it like. He's a hot commodity. Come on people! Stop being a double standard, like it's alright for a man but not a woman. In my opinion, do whatever make u happy. It's your life. I don't believe in judging people because none is perfect.

DB- Yes age doesn't make a diffidence but there is line to draw. That's too young she's old enough to be his mama smh.

CKI- What if he wants kids though? She's a little too old to be having kids.

MN- In this case no age is not just a number. This boy Is a teenager who does not know anything about life.

KW- Correct...... age is nothing but a number however age difference is another ball game!!!!!!

DA- If I was his mother she'd never made it to the altar.

RK- It all depends on the maturity level, I have met 12-year-old men and 30-year-old boys.

EMM- 25-year difference. I could not do it.

EMM- I have an issue with 7 years.

SK- You go Girl! Enjoy whatever time you have with mate. I'm not judging. All I got to say is must be nice to roll over to a nice big already ready! LOL, I AINT MADD at CHA!

AGL- Wow I think he must have turned on something that was off for a mighty long time.

JG- No what are they going to talk about the power rangers?

BP- #Later it will be!

JG- Age is a number, but it can be the wrong number! What do they have in common that they both can relate to? She has already experienced life, and his is just beginning! It's wrong for her to cheat him out of his growing and learning skills that EVERY young adult needs to go through while they're still single and free from the cares of life!!

MW- ABSOLUTELY!

JG- People talk themselves into situations, and then blame everybody but themselves for their part in their twisted thinking, to validate the "wrong- ness" of their actions! "GROW UP"!!!

EBAS- Sometimes. Depends on The Level Of Maturity.

RE- Age is just a number, but you must understand that there is a totally different level of intelligence that come with that number.

RE- Plus if I was her son it would be very hard for me to submit to a step dad who's younger than me.

GM- I think at 19 he's being robbed/deprived of life experiences, education, career growth and maturity. She's more than twice his age and has lived. If she really loved him she would set him free broken-hearted and all.... As his mother I would have a problem with her. #boytoy

LW- Me too!!

SCS- He is going to stray, eventually. His female peers are going to ridicule him, she is going to grow old well before he does, she will constantly worry about him cheating, and he is losing out on so much freedom by choosing someone that has already had a chance at her freedom. It won't work. I've been there. But my ex was the one jealous, although he was the much younger one. His immaturity kicked in when he saw older men gawking at me. He couldn't handle it. He looked for me to mother him, also. It's a true burden. They may LOOK mature, but believe me, they are very much YOUNG....

JG- YES MA'AM!!! I COULDN'T HAVE SAID THAT ANY BETTER, QUEEN SONYA!! YOU AIN'T NEVER LIED!!!

TE- He might have I need a mama issue. And she might have issues of control and need to take care of someone. We can only inquire in a few years and see if the interview is conducted one on one. Or together and if the subject is how immature he is; or how she's letting herself go. Or it might be how much they love each other. You see everyone is different and what I can't see for me might be perfect for you. So, more power to them!

DM- Maybe nothing to talk about now, till the wrinkles set in....

FM- That man is getting good some 44-year-old always wet and ready to go booby. God bless him.

BP- Example when you take #GoodSex too far...

BR- Age is but maturity is a whole different thing.

AY- Not that age. Lol

LW- Noooo! There are some circumstances where age does matter! Such as: He may want children, but she's past that stage in her life, etc...

AH- Yes nothing but a #

MW- 19 and forty-seven she better be rich.

AJS- All I can say is. Cougar.

AW- He's just a Baby!!!! No way!

KGJ- Noooo! Age is not just a number and I realize she's at an age where she can have sex without consequences of pregnancy and he's at the
right age to where all he wants to do is have sex what happens when real life steps in

CR- When real life step in he will step out smh

DT- No she is old enough to be his mother. Where is his mom?

WD- Just a number if both are legal. But I've been there before, and both need to have an understanding about kids and the Golden years.

DB- No... It can interfere with a person's natural mental growth if the gap in age is too long 🖤☐🦋☐🖤☐

PP- Not that age 19 no way 10 years difference okay.

TMW- She should be locked up after investigation. She was probably messing with him other underage boys before this.

SB- He is very young. ..but I met a couple in the store I work at. He looks to be in his early twenties and she looked around late sixties. I commented on her fabulous ring and she said he picked it, then he looked at her and said," 'anything for my wife ". Well you could have knocked me down with a feather. He had tats and some piercings, and she had purple hair. So, there is someone for everyone, and life is short. They were cute to watch and seemed enamored with each other. Who am I to judge? I hope I can find that type of Love before I die. Meanwhile, I worry more about that crazy Trump.

MC- I had a cousin who married a 19-year-old, she was 28 and I was 18 and could see it wasn't going to work.... not so much because of the age, but because his Mom and sister went on the honeymoon with them. Ridamndiculous!!!!

SM- The only reason a 44-year-old woman with a 19-year-old boy is sex. She must have a lot of negative baggage or can't find a man evenly yoke her age. He might as well enjoy the ride!
NT- Yes, when they both are responsible adults, age doesn't matter.

LJG- idk because everyone is doing it...my nephew is 30 n his gf is 18 I think its nuts n my bro. is also 10yrs diff w. his gf I feel that be with your age category because it will matter EVENTUALLY.

MC- My parents met when Mom was 16 and my Dad was 21. Isn't noooooo way, I would allow a 21-year-old to date my daughter or sons. But, hey...they were together 48 years till my Dad passed, so....

LO- He's not even a man.

FS- Turn it around, he's 44 and she's 19...what it looks like then. But him lucky at the beginning.

SN- What's ok for a man to do way younger. So, its ok when a woman does it.

JG- SMH! SHAME ON HER! SHE CLEARLY TOOK ADVANTAGE OF HIS IMMATURITY!!

JLF- Hahaha I love the sarcasm

JG- I'm being crystal clear, not sarcastic

JLF- I completely understand

JG- It's all good, King James!

TBO- Yes if He is of age. You can't stop what a person is Feeling for Another Person.

TE- If they like it I love it! People don't always come in your life to stay... sometimes they are simply there to show you something you need to know. So, if it doesn't last, they both get a life lesson that usually helps you grow as a person. IJS

JLF- To be honest I would have a hard time accepting the relationship if it were my daughter but if it were my son not so much so. It's a protective Dad kind of thing even though I have taught my daughter very well. Double Standards? Yes.

GP- She is having sex with that baby can hurt him" No!

KI- GO FOR IT !!!!!!!!!!!!!!!!!!!!!

AN- That is up to those 2 individuals.......... I'm not profiting nothing from wat decisions they make.

SH- TWO QUOTES:
1) "Let no man put asunder what GOD has joined together."
2) "It's better to have loved and lost than never to have loved at all." Some people never find someone to love so much that differences can't prevent them from growing closer. I guess a lot of you don't know, "Love is blind."

TFH- They say age doesn't make a difference, but in this case, it does. I can see if he was 7 to 10 years younger. But no way not this. Even though a lot of men have done this throughout the years. It's a no.

PC- No, until you marry your grandmother................😏☺

SJ- Nurp And She's getting HER ASS KICKED LMAO

ID- If it real what am I to say. I can't judge. My boo was 20 year my senior and we were together until death.

PG- He going to learn today 😁☐

JLF- At 19 years old we can guess why she with the young man. I can recall in my youth, darn near breaking up five homes and slowly learning the reasons and the power behind what these ladies wanted to do that I thought was ridiculous and crazy, those beautiful, stately intelligent and mature Queens were tempted and confused by the attention of a younger man. They want to leave their families and move away with a 20 to 23-year-old young man, the youngest of the five of them was 15 years my senior. Three of them quit their jobs and two temporarily left their husbands and one tried to hurt herself, I felt terrible and it changed me completely. So, you are right Ms. PG, he's going to learn.

SS-Not for me. I can understand him being infatuated, but her, I don't get. But hey I wish them luck.

MG- Depends on what I'm wanting from him.

RW- Seems to me, he is looking for a momma.

MW- She got him off layaway, this a bit much. Hmmmm!

SJ- Personally if you're only ten years older it's ok but twenty + is his mom.

KC- I believe too young is like being with a child & too old is like being with your GM or GF.

EW- Love is just a number. If the both are comfortable with it. (Go for it) my opinion.

KM- To some age is just a number knowing where a person mentality is all what done care. But me.... Ummmm no I couldn't do it cause his age puts him like he's my son.... Nope I'll pass.

KING-ISMS

We tend not to deviate from the norm, which means not having partners with a wide age gap from our own. However, some seem to make it work while others fall back and start over. Going through life while searching for the perfect relationship can be tough. More so, when there seems to be a small wedge from the start, that's when we get to consider new perspectives and find new meaning within ourselves and others.

Statistics back up the basis for not getting into a relationship with a significant age gap difference, but as of now let's be somewhat neutral and a wee bit personal. And really, we're not here to look at the formula on how to realize the socially acceptable age for a relationship, which is your age divided by two plus seven...not really. C'mon who has time for that?

Age does matter, no matter what other people think; they tend to assume just because you're happy, it also means you're contented. Just because there's chemistry means it's what we've been looking for. There are different layers that people in love tend not to see and happiness is just one of them. You can't build a relationship on happiness alone. It needs a lot of work to keep it together, and there is no couple out there who doesn't have some sort of a problem, which eventually gets settled. Those who say they don't have to re-evaluate themselves and their bond don't understand that's what a working relationship looks like ...it's a messy joyous coupling.

People conclude that just because they are a few years apart, those years should be considered an age difference. Age won't matter if the gap isn't as wide as you think; there is a difference between talking about what movies are considered the best in the last few years and what it was like to live in a world where the best thing that existed was dial-up internet. Not to mention political viewpoints, future, relatable friends, music and all the things in-between that round up a relationship. The day-to-day events couples experience together can make a huge difference. The tendency is that one of the partners will be unhappy if there is too great a gulf.

Some blooming adolescents have mature thinking patterns while some adults have a tender way of thinking and that's all right, for now. It doesn't have to be a "meeting of the minds" all the time. People tend to fall just because. Doesn't everybody long for a stable and long-lasting relationship? When some people fall into love, they really do fall into love. In a perfect world, that's enough to last and such an attitude usually falls under the "I don't care what other people think" category. Don't get me wrong, I have no issue with that. I will personally salute you for that. But like I said, your emotions aren't the only factor in a relationship. If you can find the same passion, likes, and dislikes, then, go ahead, but that raging attraction alone is not enough to sustain a committed lifestyle in long-coming years. Even the best of us fall out of love for menial things, like if one or the other is looking ahead to the future, while their partner is still stuck in the present.

Your Answer

CHAPTER 10

Do all women look at another woman's butt?

QUESTION: Do all women look at another woman's butt?

PP- Wow I hope not but I do give women compliments.

KCP- Then you are looking at her ass!

PP- No I'm not looking at her butt I give a woman a compliment when she's well-dressed I don't care how her but look lol

KCP- Yes you are...own up!

PP- And if I want to look at a nice butt I'll get in the mirror and look at my own and give myself a compliment.

KCP- Yea Right!

DA- Yes, we do. Not in a ooooo (drool drool) way but in a she looks good in that or a she knows her butt too big for that way.

KCP- 😂😂😂😂😂😂😂😂 lol

RG- Yes and no. If Its hour glass shaped stand out can't help. But to see it they want u to see it. Some pull their blouse up in the back guy asked did I have implants. No sir no disrespect. I have she kill me she walks she have a car hip and the butt. And the looks and bootlegged. And found what men like. She does it on purpose she laughing I taught her to walk a certain way. she wants boom patty cake. Lawd help us. Lol

KCP- What the hell are you talking about? Take your medication!

CKI- I know I do. Not in a sexual way, but more like admiration.

TR- Most likely if they aren't blind of course I have but not in a sexual desiring way.

SM- I do. Not able to speak for the others. Lol #nohomo

KWF- Yes but not in a desiring way but in a complimentary way OR a disgusting way.

LH- Yes if you have it you have it. I am looking.

LRG- duh!!! 😊

MG- Yes, I do especially when they have on tight dresses with a lot of hell Damage I like does she not see that.

BR- Yes, we do comparisons.

LC- Sure. I think we check each other out all the time, and not in a sexual manner. They always say that women dress for other women. Girl, I love your.....

AY- All the time.

SA- Yes, I do, am a personal trainer so it's just habit!

TS- Aaahhhh...yes on the DL. They size each other up. We're very competitive. If her body is better, we'll find ways to point out flaws about her.

EBS- If You're Not A Dude, Your Butt Doesn't Interested Me at All.
CC- I agree with you.

DM- Yes, we do, we look at the hair legs, breasts, how big they stomach. we look at everything. We need something to compare ourselves to. But I personally don't look😊☐😊☐😊☐

DB- Yes lol not in a sexual matter.

MJ- Yes, will tell her she looks nice. I am very sure of me. So, I think we as females should up lift each other up.

SJ- Yepper we Just looking to see how that outfit Fitting lol

TMS- Yes because if its right and tight, then please tell me what I need to Do😊☐Building and Complementing One Queen at a Time.

LJG- always check everybody out from head to toe...because I love to see what people are wearing n their shape. Just because I like too..

JH- I look at everybody...non-sexual of course...especially hair and shoes...nonjudgmental, just observant. I compliment everybody as well.

LS- Yes, but not in the same manner that men do, at least I don't!

CA- Yes with no hesitation!

ABW- Yes indeed because sometimes I say I wish mine looked like hers!

SV- Of course and I compliment them as well.

ST- Yea and I compliment them if the carry themselves well.
BO- Yes, but not lusting. Just giving credit where credit is due.

BR- Yup, I do. It's just a habit!

DT- Yes but not in a I want to get with that!!!

DG- Of course woman check each other out that's natural.

TCJ- Yes rather hating or complimenting.

DG- I do!!! Heck I like shape and styling people, so I look and compliment!!!

DS- Yes. No homo but yes!

SK- AND GIVE CREDIT WHERE ITS DUE!

DR- So why u get mad when we do it?

SB- Who's mad?

JH- Lusting is different Mr. DR! Lol

DR- No I'm talking about looking some women get mad when u look and u know it's true

DD- Depends on what you are wearing.

KING-ISMS

They stare, they ogle, they pat, and they pinch. But what is it that draws some women so intensely to the female behind? The long-held theory that an hourglass figure, including a full lower body, is attractive because it suggests health and fertility has been largely discredited. It has yet to be replaced by a convincing alternative. What we do know is that a booty is a uniquely female trait—and therefore uniquely feminine.

After puberty, sex hormones begin to dictate the distribution of fat on the body. In men, fat accumulation is stimulated around the gut and inhibited in the seat. It's the opposite for women, who tend to carry fat in their gluteo-femoral region, that is, the butt and thighs.

And, other women's eyes tend to get stuck on other women's asses!

Your Answer

I Don't Have the Answers, But I Do Have Some Questions

CHAPTER 11

Would you stay with your mate that has contracted HIV through a blood transfusion?

QUESTION: Would you stay with your mate that has contracted HIV through a blood transfusion?

EBAS- I Would Have to Seriously Pray. That I Would Have The compassion To Say Yes.

QGB- I hear you Queen

JH- It should be a mutual decision

JH- Okay, so what if she/he breaks off the relationship and no matter what reassurances you give them they're determined to end things?

QGB- If the person with the HIV decided to end thing's on no uncertain terms, it's then Over! In no circumstances can you force anyone to stay with you!

EBAS- You Are Free to Leave If They Aren't Please to Dwell with You. It's for Better or Worse but You Still Have Something Called Freewill. Great Response King

JH- Noted

RE- For better or worse. Can we keep our promise?

RC- Hell no!

KG- If I am married and my husband becomes sick and contracts this disease due to a transfusion I would stand by his side. Till death do us part, for better or for worse.

DX- I am certified professional phlebitis I haven't been in a while but the mistake itself is a huge possible lawsuit, those pills are expensive.

JW- That's a tough question? I would have to do a lot of praying. There's a lot to consider.

TJ- What is there to risk??? You educate yourself on HIV & you support the person you claim to love. The end!

SN- Yes, until death do us part. Taking your vows in front of God is serious business.

DB- I would have to pray about it.

CA- When I travel through Black America and see setups for HIV testing, I am highly offended; when was the last time you saw this in North Dallas or any other place predominantly white? You have not seen it; moreover, we do not see Hispanics being tested for HIV, why? I know many , like believing in the false Jesus, will think this a lie, but when you look at it, you not only find that it's a like but also that it does not make sense: How many Blacks or any other people have died from AIDS who had never been tested for HIV ? there are not any, and all of those who have died from it, were first tested, does that make sense? how is it that we have a virus killing people, but only kills those who have been tested for it ? would we not find somebody dead somewhere as a result of AIDS virus who refused to be tested ? Black America and all my brothers and sisters, if you are never tested, you will never die from AIDS because it has nothing to do with what's in your body that kills you, it's what they give you after telling you that you are HIV positive, and it's all designed to further genocide against Black America; ironically, in order to make it seem logical or real, they kill off a few whites and others, but the objective is to remove Blacks from the face of the earth, and when we believe in AIDS or HIV encouraging others to be tested, we're conspiring genocide against ourselves !

CKI- I guess I'm a gonner then I've been tested three times twice at the OBGYN and once at a mobile clinic

SN- That was not the question. It makes me sad, knowing that when you die, you're going to hell. Jesus is very real!!

CKI- Huh? Who is going to hell?

EBAS- Me too Sister Queen I Been with One Man for The Last 34 Years and Trust Me I Get Tested. And If the Next Man Enter This Temple He Must Be Tested.

CKI- Man now I'm going to be paranoid that I have it...since I've been tested before. I wish I hadn't read this comment.

EBAS- Child Please Trust God.

QGB- Thinking about your words King CA about being tested at those mobile sites and suddenly you have the HIV virus, makes too much freaking sense! Y'all think about it, they're totally fine before they go get themselves checked out at these sites; but then leave away sick with this virus. Wow! Now on the other note; My Jesus is real; the Lord is real to me. Your thoughts about him is truly yours King, yet our beliefs in Christ Jesus belongs to those who do! Let's respect one another's views on this subject; and continue to agree to disagree! Respectfully.

EBAS- Sad But True If HIV Don't Take You Out the Medication Will. I've Seen in My Medical Profession People Are Devastated by The Cost and Possible Side Effect from Those Meds.

LDD- Yes....if my man contracted HIV thru a transfusion till death do us part with precautions of course...!

CA- You are a good woman, be blessed!

CKI- We'd stay together, but I don't know if we'd be having sex though.

LS- Yes, because I know that God is bigger than HIV. I am not trying to be all holy, but I am just keeping it real. Just my opinion!

KB- YES...most definitely indeed, the question was answered when you said king or queen!!! That's something that goes down without even having to think about it, we made vows to one another, till death, richer poorer, sickness and in health!!! That's nonnegotiable 24 7 365!!!

EDD- Yes! HIV isn't a death sentence anymore. Protect myself with education and condoms, she makes sure she is taking all of the necessary medications and we love life together.

VV- Yes if I was very educated on the disease no matter what I will stick with them.

DB- Absolutely... No risk when you take all precautions that must be taken 🖤☐👑☐

PA- Sickness or health till death do us part I'm there 👑☐

EE- I'd be in line for my shot and bag of monthly pills UNCONDITIONAL VOWS LIFE OR DEATH= RIDE or DIE!

QGB- Wow, now that's truth in love and forever...Smiling

DW- Yes if he is my husband.

CA- I am sorry it took so long, but I am just now seeing your response: I have tried to tell others for years, there is "No HIV" to kill anybody; this whole HIV hoax was taken from Africa about a two-hundred- years ago based on witch doctor's practices; as you know, Africans lived in tribes and had witch doctors; in addition, there were taboos or social prohibitions for tribal members to follow, and if one violated one or more of the social prohibitions, he or she was tried before the witch doctor, and if found guilty, the sentence could be "Death before sunrise!" European scientists studied this for many years, and they were afraid of it because the tribal member always died just before sunrise as the witch doctor pronounced; this was very puzzling to European scientists until they found out, "There is an Inverse relationship between Fear and Immunity, which means that the more fearful we become, the weaker our immune system becomes, so what is man's greatest fear ? is it not death ? therefore, when the witch doctor pronounced death before sunrise, the tribal member was overwhelmed with the fear of dear, and the closer morning came, the tribal member became more fearful of death! I am taught that the tribal member would go through three stages: 1. Fight or Flight; meaning he would try to defeat the threat of death or out-run it to escape it, and whether fighting or running, he enters stage 2. Exhaustion; then the last stage 3. Death, is this not the same as HIV testing? the person is told, "You are HIV Positive and have about two years to live; as you know, there is no cure, but we can give you something to treat it," is that not correct? The something given to them as treatment is, Antigens which further activates and depletes the immune system; this is the cause of death for those having been given the HIV Positive results, but if you are never tested, you could live to be a hundred or more because HIV is a hoax contributing to genocide of Black people!

ID- Make sure you know the history on HIV, give your support, always stay upon it educate yourself

GJH- O WOW this is Deep.

SK- I can't ANWSER that one. I don't want to face that one. Or have to confront it.

CA- I will drink the blood of anyone professed to have HIV in order to prove what I am saying, and if I did not know, I would not say it; again, it's the "Antigens" given as treatment that's killing our brothers and sisters all over the world, it's legal murder, but if you don't ever be tested or given the alleged treatment, you will never die from this hoax called AIDS; think about it, only a fool would believe there is a virus killing people, but it only kills those who are tested and treated, does that make sense? Why wouldn't we find some dead from it who did not go to
be tested? Scripture teaches us that only 144,000 will be saved, so whit that in mind, we see the wickedness in our world, but it's God who gives wisdom knowledge and understanding, and when we believe in God, we believe in and seek wisdom knowledge and understanding; we have many brothers and sisters who are ignorant as a result of slavery; they are dying from false diagnosis of "Prostate Cancer"; AIDS; Breast Cancer; Diabetes; High Blood Pressure and a host of other things that have nothing to do with their health, it's all about genocide, beware !

EC- Why is god only saving 144,000. What happens to the rest of the world that is serving god the way they should. What are you saying... God has a lottery?

CA- No, God does not have a lottery; God gave the choice to us when he told us, "This day, I set before you both good and evil, you choose" ; do we not see 99.9% choosing evil? then what about God's word, "Thy shall have no other God before me;" do we not hear more Blacks calling on Jesus than God? did not God tell us, "Besides me, there is no other? did God not tell us, "Cursed is he that believes in man, and is not this fictitious Jesus a man? what rest of the world is serving God? No one can be serving God who does not obey the Word of God, and I cannot know if they are serving God or not unless I hear them call on Jesus, a false God; in answer to your question, that's why only 144, 000 will be saved?

EC- So CA, what you're telling me is that with the billions of people around the world that are TRULY serving god, he will only pick 144,000? What happens to the rest of them? I understand what's going on in this world and that a lot of people aren't serving god like we should be including me. If it's like that what's the use of serving god if you might not be one of the 144,000 chosen. The same way that I don't understand, how god kicked cane of the land after killing his brother, gets branded on the forehead gets his own land and a woman??? THATS NOT FAIR OF GOD TO BLESS A KILLER BECAUSE THATS WHAT HE DID.

CA- You are referring to a Myth, not the word of God; have you sought God with all your heart and mind, or have you accepted what you have been told and profess to love Jesus? We cannot say how many people are serving God else we would be God, but we can say, those who call on a fictitious Jesus are not serving God because God tells us, "Thy shall have no other God before me," did he not say that? moreover, did God not say, I am the first and the last, and besides me there is no other? did God not say that? then where did this false Jesus come from? are not those who profess to love Jesus disobeying the Word of God; always know, anything that is not fair is not of God, be blessed !

CA- I cannot say enough about this because I know there are many Blacks who don't believe the truth because they do not think, and when you don't think, you do not use reasoning to reach conclusions about anything: This HIV or AIDS don't make sense: God says, "Come now, let us reason together...," Isiah 1:18; reasoning involves questioning and answering by using inductive and deductive reasoning: How can a people be foolish enough to believe that people are dying from a virus called HIV or AIDs but don't die before they are tested?

KING-ISMS

Are all relationships affected by HIV doomed? Break-ups can happen for reasons that have nothing to do with HIV, but sometimes it does play a part, especially if you have been newly diagnosed, or if you were infected outside your relationship.

There are plenty of reasons why a relationship might be kept going after it has run its course. An HIV negative partner might think that they can't leave because it would look like they were abandoning their partner. The person living with HIV would be left without support when they needed it. They would feel guilty or worry that their partner wouldn't find someone else. As the HIV positive partner, you might stay because: You worry about not being able to find another relationship. You might feel guilty at wanting to leave your partner.

Should I stay in my current relationship no matter what? Everyone is capable of loving and being loved, regardless of their HIV status. If the main thing keeping two people together is guilt, pity, or fear of loneliness this is not healthy for either partner. If you're unhappy with the relationship for whatever reason, the chances are your partner will be too sooner or later.

Your Answer

CHAPTER 12

Is a man potentially on the DL if he likes and wants anal sex with his wife?

QUESTION: Is a man potentially on the DL if he likes and wants anal sex with his wife?

CJ- This is an excellent question, I am going to wait for some responses on this topic! Hmmmmmm

TS- Anal is NOT my thing!!! Ooh my...I can't answer this one and neither will I try😱😱😱

TS- I'm outta this one...I'm just gonna sit this one out ok😄😄😄

PL- My mom used to say "Opinions are just like A--holes, everybody has one...So here's my opinion, not necessarily. BUT, if that is all he can think about, and every time you get in the bed he's flipping you over, you better start doing some serious contemplating on that dude...

VQ- Exactly

EBAS- Show You Right PL.

EBAS- I Want All or Nothing DL Brothers Need Not To Apply...

CKI- If he prefers anal to vaginal maybe.

MC- Suspect. .no ma'am PB not Wayman! I know every line in the movie...Bernaaaard! Oh Shame!

BM- No but make u think.

MC- What if he only wants BJ's could say the same, no?

KC- Don't be trying to criticize the BJ's

MC- Ok King C, I know what YOU like to do!

EW- I think he can think of something better than anal sex. (My opinion)

QGB- I ain't playing! Uggggghhhh

JB- Ummmm...Yes

JB- Wait is he receiving?

MW- Whatever works for them kings, some queens, but to me an ass hole, is an asshole, man or woman so I stay out lol...

KC- For Real!

MC- This reminds me of a story that someone told me a long time ago this woman was married to this man and he had boyfriends and girlfriend and she wasn't even mad because he was just like insatiable and she was like this gives me a rest. SMH.

DB- No... However, if that's his only and most frequent preference then yes, he's DL I would say♥☐🐾☐

SK- I Don't know what to make of that. I'm not into that one.

CB- Well F.B. as my Grand Father would say back in his day; If you have sex with a woman in the Booty, you might as well have sex with a man in The Booty...Because "Booty Hole is Booty Hole" To me he's so right, Simple fact, now day's you can never tell especially late night in the club. Half-drunk hole, is hole. For Myself It's "PERVERTED." Oh, by the way Donald Trump finally came Out the Closet.😂❓😋❓😂☐😷☐😎☐

LDD- I can't answer because that's out of my scope of participation........!

MJ- Not sure because some women like anal sex.

CB- But still, it's not natural. Who wants a Like Me a 12in Python going up in their Booty? Hell, it's bad enough that a woman let me put it where it's intended ... Just Saying...😎☺😃❓😅🙂 🙂😅 😎

MJ- Thanks CB, I needed a good laugh 😅❓😅🙂😅🙂😅🙂😂🙂😂🙂

SH- NO! Some women like insist on it, some are afraid it might hurt too much. Giving those who like it what they like don't make a man gay or have gay tendencies. He's manning up for his lady and enjoying the ride, pun intended. It's just another feminine hole to get off in... more pun intended. Being gay is the only thing that makes a man gay. If you aren't gay can't nothing make you're a&& gay, punk insinuated.

CK- No, just not my thang

BWT- Make me wonder don't it! Closet Gay!

CA- I am not clear on what DL means; however, I can respond to the question about anal sex with wife or girlfriend, and even though I know some women profess to like it, I think it's a sick man who would do that to his girlfriend or wife; it's abnormal, and even "dogs" don't do that!

JMS- ABSOLUTELY! I say that because that ish is Un-natural. Plain and simple

LSM- Hell yeah that's how that Spirit get started men want to go behind because they feel like it's smaller and Tighter and their start Desiring that instead of what they supposed to be Desiring and that's a female vagina they start saying that the female vagina is too big so they want to go behind because it's smaller n tighter lol I'm sorry for being so blunt but I'm a woman that just keep it real.

MF- hmmm it never occurred to me to think that automatically. It could be, or maybe he tried it with women and liked it.

KING-ISMS

Some guys are boobs men. Others are legs men. But in the bedroom, all are ass men. I do not know a heterosexual woman alive who has not, at some point, experienced a partner trying to use her backdoor instead of the front. There are the curious gents, gently investigating if the key fits. Others are as unsubtle as the pile of junk mail flyers that stumbles through your letterbox every week. But the male's goal is the same: they want in! I know plenty of women who've tried anal play, but I don't know one who initiated it – or who'd admit to it without that other essential lubricant, wine.

"It's all that internet porn men are watching," I hear you cry – and, yes, true. Over the last six years, PornHub has reported a 78% increase in the number of searches for anal clips. Long ago, a time before a phone could send a photo let alone stream PornHub – guys' drunken banter still involved cheers of "Up the ass, no harm done!" The irony was that most were virgins and had little idea how to handle a vagina, heaven forbid anything more complex. Still, they wanted to. That's the allure of the ass. But if porn and peer pressure are only half the motivation, what's the rest? I am going to break down men's fascination with the hole-y grail of sex. And, oh my, it's interesting.

At its most basic, men crave novelty more than women. If a woman finds something that she likes sexually, she usually wants that repeated and again. Whereas men seem to need different stimuli to stay engaged. The anus and anal sex is more taboo than vaginal sex; it's perceived as 'dirty'. If a woman is open to it, it implies that your sex life is 'dirtier', too." And 'dirty' is a label that novelty-addicted guys crave – not fear.

Anal sex avoids intimacy – cue the commitment-phobes.

The most common position in anal sex is for the woman to be bent over, with the man on top or over her, looking at her back. For men, a sense of power and domination comes with that. There's also no real connection: there's no face-to-face interaction, no eye contact, it avoids intimacy and is not seen as a 'relationship experience'. In our culture, men's emotions are more suppressed than women's. So, men might find anal sex more comfortable because of the lack of intimacy, while women might find it less satisfying because of the same thing."

Your Answer

CHAPTER 13

What is the difference between opinions and judging?

QUESTION: What's the difference between opinions and judging?

GP- Having an open mind' judgment free

SK- UDGING TO ME IS CRITCIZING SOMEONE ELSE. NOW DICUSSING SOMETHING SHOULD BE OPNINION ONLY. ARE USE SELF AS EXAMPLE.

JLF- No preconceived notions or ideas open for discussion and without condemnation but it's such a thin line because it can become patronizing when you omit your experiences. Damn good question. Without looking it up.

JW- When you judge someone normally you don't have all the facts about what you're talking about, so you are giving your opinion...discussion is when you are open to finding a solution to whatever you are talking about.

DDM- Judging is pointing the finger at somebody else unrighteous (one sided), a discussion is more than one person stating their own opinions on a matter and resolving it together.

EE- Discussion is tossing ideas and onions around without a right or wrong outcome judging is making definitive resolutions based on facts or opinions of one or more people against another person or group.

KKD- Yes judgment is something I try not to do. When I discuss something it's my proof for me. What's good for you may not be good for me, but I can't tell you what's best for you or look down on you.

TE- I don't believe that you must necessarily come to an agreement so per say with a discussion. You are simply stating your thoughts and opinions and you listen to and respect the thoughts a belief of others. You can agree to disagree in the end. I don't have to believe what the other person says but I should respect it. But when you start telling people they are going to hell because they wear red socks or because they don't conform to your way of thinking that's being judgmental.
DDM- Not necessarily coming to an agreement but ending it without it escalating.

TE- Yes ma'am you are right Queen! That is always best.

AJS- The difference is. Real street talk. Judging is pointing and individual out and slanting his are her character. No facts at all. Discussion is talking about an individual with one are two more people's opinions. That's the street version of them two.

MC- To me it's like when someone says: that didn't make any sense....no, it doesn't make sense to YOU! WE ALL get caught up at some point or another. Have empathy. if you GOTTA speak on the person offer help or advice in the next breath, act, or better yet, say a prayer.

KPS- Judging is based on your own prejudices; discussion is a fair exchange of ideas.

VJ- Well said! I think judging can also be based on individual's beliefs (religious)

RE- One attacks someone's character. The other speaks of themselves.

LO- One is preconceived whereas the other is open minded

MJ- If the person you and whoever is discussing in the conversation also. If any advice is given is it constructive or Is it vicious.

PW- Judging is talking about someone or something without any evidence, just slander based on you own opinion, a discussion is listening to other opinions.

CA- Judging is having reached a conclusion or defined another or others character as such and such; whereas a discussion is just that, to talk about a person or anything without defining it as such and such!

CF- Discussing something should be an opinion. Judging is criticizing.

AY- It's like hearing both sides, the ones that judges usually are the ones that has their mine made up end of discussion. So, before you judge listen, before you discuss have an open mind. Facts over fiction.

ID- Judging is making it law. Discussing is coming up with the reason why.

JG- This word his highly misused and misunderstood. Because of its various uses. The negative way it us used is when it is used to condemn or shame someone. When the individual that is judging someone is guilty of things themselves. Which applies to everyone. But there are instances where we must make a judgement not to condemn or find anyone guilty but to discover truth. Like many things it's all about delivery.

KING-ISMS

The words criticism and judgment are highly charged in our culture. In part, we have lost the ability to not only be discerning but unhappy. The ability to express what is being discerned clearly is primarily understood out of fear of "offending". We live in a society increasingly concerned with political correctness and avoiding "offense" rather than seeing through into the heart of the issue that is "intellectualism".

When you use the term criticism, are you really referring to passing judgment? I suspect you are. In my opinion, we have lost the ability to discern between the two. . . criticism is an essential aspect of critical thinking. And, critical thinking is sorely missing in our society. Knowing when and how to give "constructive" feedback is a skill that very people are taught. Combined with a society in an era that cares less about character, integrity, and authenticity this confusion you reinforce leads to increased dumbing down, and dismissal of *any* expression of criticality as "intellectualism" or merely, "offensive".

Perhaps you could write another article extolling the virtue of critical thinking and the use of intelligence to discern to encourage people to have the courage to be more discerning and to speak out when they see things that are wrong - not to stand in judgment, not to be violent, but to bring light into situations.

We need more critical discernment, not less.

Your Answer

I Don't Have the Answers, But I Do Have Some Questions

CHAPTER 14

If a man/woman is legally separated, is it wrong for them to date?

QUESTION: If a Man/Woman is Legally Separated, is it Wrong for Them to Date?

KAB- Depends on how DEVOUT ONE IS!

RT- Nope! Okay! Bye!

KG- In the eye sight of God they are wrong.

LBS- He would still be off limits because legally separated is still married!

JLF- is it fair?

CA- Yes of course it is wrong. Until he or she gets a divorce because she or he still have legal to receive the benefits of his or her life.

FK- Lol, syke... this is the way my ex feels. I left him two years ago and he still complaining that I am his and he still has rights to me. For the 15 years we were together he should have taken advantage of it then. One of our main problems was his low testosterone that he would not get help for it. People think that having low testosterone just gives a person a low sex drive. But having low testosterone does a lot more to a person mentally and it really messes up a marriage. But on top of this guy being bipolar and schizophrenic I had to leave!

CA- Okay I'm not a counselor but if you still married to him he still belongs to you and you still belongs to him the Bible says for the good or the bad pray about his physical problem in his mental problem and see what God the action does not to be reactive not to be bitter towards our soulmates

FD- Biblically speaking yes, they are off limits.

MC- Excuse my language but HELL TO THE YES!!!!😡☐😡☐😡☐😡☐

MW- MORALY AND LEGALLY YES! BUT I'M GOING TO MIND MY BUSINESS. HMMMM! LOL,

JD- Yes, as he/she is in a holding pattern. Hold means not able to go forward or backward. A person should be able to move forward.

JJ- Ok people y'all say in God eyes she's still married I feel she still married in Gods eyes because your vows r until death do u apart so that not in God eyes that's man words so in God eyes a divorce make u single in man eyes not God so don't get it twisted just my opinion love and peace

SH- Yes get Divorce first regardless there still married.

PB- Yes, the person need to get a divorce before getting involved with another person okay.

PB- yes you cannot move forward in life and still have baggage OK.

QGB- If there is not an active divorce pending, yes you should steer clear! No need in setting yourself up, in case there's a change of heart! Smiling.

PA- Someone is already being off limits most of the time causing the separation👑☐

TC- Yes! He's not Divorce in the eyes of God and Law he's still marry. That's FACT can't water down that.

MS- Yes. Too much drama. Still not divorced. Separated people get back together sometimes. That's a NO GO

EBAS- It probably is okay in my opinion especially if you are really planning on moving to the next step which is divorce

Gm- Off-limits. You must be free to move forward in another relationship for it to be happy healthy

IR- He will 4ever be off limits I would never set eyes on him.

CH- It's obvious their still committed to each other at the heart.......... so, the separation must be for financial reasons....

CJD- Yep. No such thing as no "legal separation" anymore. Either yo ass is IN or OUT #PERIOD. Don't want someone else's property. I want my OWN. Not still attached to another. Show me DIVORCE papers. Then I'll take you SERIOUSLY ✌

MR- Even if there's a divorce pending you both do not have the right to date or have a relationship you make the next person and adultery just as you are, and it will be consequences in the name of Jesus Christ so stay clear until final papers and payments are done each party can use it in court in the state of Texas.

CB- no, waiting on divorce settlements can take forever and tomorrow is not promised.

IM- Must enjoy life while u can!!!

TP- He just became a BIGGER HOE 😁☐😁☐😁☐

KPS- Separation can mean many things...separated and working it out...separated to be divorced...separated and living separated...each case is taken separately in my opinion...so no she isn't off limits

DR- YES, Waaaaay off limits.

SM- YES ACCORDING TO THE MARITAL AGREEMENT, BUT IF IT WERE I...I WOULD HAVE TO IMMEDIATELY RUN BACK TO THE COURT'S AND REVERSE SOME THINGS ADMITTING THAT I F'ED UP! BESIDES WHO

WANTS TO HAVE THEIR LIFE TIED UP WITH SOMEONE THAT YOU SHARE NOTHING ELSE IN COMMON WITH!

KAB- I've never been Married because I've NEVER BEEN RIGHT WITH GOD...I'm 42yrs. I'm engaged 2 a Man who LOVES THE LORD B4 HE LOVES ME! We'll be 2gether 2yrs. this March. I've been DRUG & THE LIFESTYLE FREE 4 7YRS.! This is the 1st time I've EVER BEEN IN LOVE WITH ANYONE! I LOVE THE LORD B4 I LOVE him...I believe THE WORD & N THE GOOD BOOK, THERE IS NO DIVORCE! These R TROUBLE TIMES where PEOPLE have put the BIBLE AWAY & treat MARRIAGE as a HOOK-UP till things go SOUTH then decide they made a "MISTAKE MARRYING" so, "NO BIGGIE...WE'LL DIVORCE"...This is NOT what GOD PLANNED 4 US! His word says MARRIAGE IS A COVENANT BETWEEN ONE WOMAN & ONE MAN! I could go on & on, but I'm NOT a preacher, just a MESSENGER. GOD BLESS & HELP US ALL...AMEN

SH- Yes only because it's my opinion that during the time you wait on a divorce, you need that time to heal and spend time being by yourself. You shouldn't just move so fast from one relationship to the next. That's your alone time with God to work on YOU!

RV- But Queen God put barriers in place for a reason, true you need your me time and time with God. But every situation is different if she's showing me that it's closure going on then. I am praying about it as I move forward, to get my Queen one-man loss is another man treasure.

EBAS- My Sister I Really Prayed About My Previous Response. Thank God for The Holy Ghost and Personal Conviction. I'm Changing My Response to Absolutely No.

RV- I respect all your sentiments, but that's like so many of you all saying, I am waiting for God to send me a good man/woman, this can be God talking to you, but letting you put in the rest of the work. Why do y'all say he don't judge then.ljs

MW- Well I am in this situation right now. Now I can say for me that I am talking with a gentleman right now but will not go beyond that if I am married. Unlike my soon to be ex.

EBAS- My Beautiful friend. And WOG Be Careful I'm in your Same Situation. Safe Guard Your Anointing. We Are Still Human. But, Nothing Is Hidden In God's Eyesight. Stay Blessed.

HTKJ- Yes, he is off the GAME unfinished business until he signs the dotted line!

DGT- No. Why not begin to get acquainted? it could go on for years the separation.

PP- If a man is legally separated yes, I think it's okay for him to date other women

SM- No...it doesn't even have to be a legal separation... it's time to move on...

GJD- HOW DO YOU BE LEGALLY SEPERATED YOU EITHER DIVORCED OR YOU NOT

CA- GJD asked a good question!

KING-ISMS

Relationships have become extremely complicated nowadays, and they really shouldn't be. People are marrying less, divorcing more, and settling for effortless, no-strings-attached situations. I am not married, nor have I ever been married. And as unconventional of a person as I may think I am, there are some things that I still find sacred. Things such as marriage, dating, and the values of family. I'm old-fashioned when it comes to courtships, and even more traditional when it comes to marriage. I want a union that is highly valued and sacred to both myself and my wife. I want to walk into a lifetime commitment with someone knowing that we meant the vows we spoke aloud.

However, as I get older and more in tune with the dating behaviors of today, I realize that not only is the way we date changing, but also the way we handle the ups and downs of marriage. There was a debate that arose on Twitter recently. A user made a point of saying that once you're married, you stay married until death or a legal divorce. They claimed that even when you're legally separated, it still means you're married. But I know some couples who don't wait for the ink to dry, choosing to date other people when they're separated. Such decisions started me thinking about how often this happens. Is it okay to date around and dance around the idea of starting a new life with someone when you haven't even closed the door on your marriage? Dating, while separated, is (not can be) difficult and comes with much drama.

Sitting in the lounge at work, a co-worker randomly shared with me that she's involved with a married man. I didn't know how to react, but she said it boldly as if it were nothing. An achievement to be proud of in a way. She disclosed that when they first started dating, she had no idea that he was married. Now that she knows, it hasn't changed her opinion or shifted her status in terms of being involved with him. She shared with me how he left his wife and children to move in with her and her children. He uses her car as if it were his own and drops her off at work most days. And as I sat and listened to her drama-filled story of the children caught in the middle (both his and hers), the man's battles with his wife who "doesn't want to let go," the house pop-ups and the vandalized property, I couldn't help but look at her with a sour taste in my mouth. Nothing about her situation seemed stable, which is more reason not to date a man who hasn't tied up his loose ends.

If the relationship is truly over between a wedded couple, the marriage should and will end in divorce. By legally separating, it means, in my opinion, that some things are still being shared between a married couple. Reconciliation is still possible. Dating while separated can also be messy because an individual might not be ready to start dating again. For some of us, when we are fresh out of a relationship, we are eager to start anew. We are anxious to get back out there and explore. But deep down, when the dust settles, we might not even be ready emotionally to invest in someone new right away. A person battling the same feelings during a separation hasn't given themselves time to learn the lessons their defunct marriage has laid out for them: Why did my marriage fail? What could I have done differently? Can we fix it? How will I do things differently in the future?

Some don't take the time to search for these answers before jumping into a courtship with someone else. Some find the answers after they already started dating again and end up right back with their estranged spouse.

The same reason you shouldn't rush into another relationship after a failed one is even more of reason, to me, to avoid dating while separated. Don't get me wrong, for those of you who have tried it, it may have worked for you. But my question is, why not just get a divorce before putting yourself back out there? After seeing your marriage crumble after all the work and love you put into it, what's the rush to do this love thing all over again?

Your Answer

CHAPTER 15

When he proposes and she doesn't Accept, is the relationship over?

QUESTION: When he Proposes and doesn't Accept, is the Relationship Over?

MC- Not necessarily. timing may not be right or the reason he is proposing may be wrong.

CM- I'm out..

KD- No not necessarily.

JWL- Pretty much a done deal

LBS- Not necessarily!! She could feel that it is too soon to get married or they could have some things to work out.

DB- Not necessarily, she loves him but may have some things to take care of.

MN- No, she just needs a little more time.

JB- Yes it should be over for as I am concerned

LK- Ask her lol

MCT- For REAL" IT JUST BEGAN???" (smile)" it's never all about you???' NOW HERE COME A REAL RELATIONSHIP. NOW???" EACH OTHER REALLY GOING KNOW TRUTH" NOW"

MF- yes, no need to waste your breath, money, or time if she doesn't want to spend her life with you.

MS- It depends on why she didn't accept it and is her reason valid.

GJ- No but never again.

TC- Yes, it's a done deal for me. We're talking about an engagement, not walking down the Aisle in 24hrs. There wouldn't be any excuses that could be said, the only thing, there could be is that you didn't love me enough to say Yes!!

CL- Not really. Either the timing isn't right, or she isn't ready for commitment just yet

DS- Why she would not accept. Something to Ponder on.

TA- No maybe she's not ready or think he's not ready.

BT- I got more game than Milton Bradley & Parker Bros if I propose and get rejected that's my gain and yo loss hearts heal now I'm desperately seeking Susan

SJ- Yepper Some Brotha's can't except rejection.

MM- Yes because they are not on the same page different signals are being sent.

RR- If u gone walk on my Luv, please take off your shoes!!!

CW- Over....done I would not ask again.

MM- That doesn't always end the relationship. Maybe that isn't a priority for her now. She may want to be sure of her commitment and security.

KPS- The relationship can continue if it was a "timing" refusal. If she refused and it's because she doesn't love him...or he got caught in a lie, IT'S OVER!

JM- Maybe he needs to just up his game and steer his thinking towards her. lol

KHJ- If I've brought myself to propose and get rejected... I feel resentment would build and I couldn't concentrate like I could before on her. I'd get in my head as to why she isn't ready...who is blocking my blessing!?

DB- It should be...❤️☐💍☐💐

CA- Not really!!! It all depends what the circumstances is when she won't marry me, so I will say it for me and no I will not stay in the relationship

LS- No, but it may be awkward for a while. He may feel rejected & start questioning the relationship, so it might cause a lil rough patch, but they can still make it thru.

MW- No! If her reason for not wanting to be a valet point and he loves her he will accepted her answer for now.

YPP- I think it just depends...is 5 weeks, 5 months, or 5 years lol

DGT- No. I don't think so. If old gal didn't want him she wouldn't wait to a proposal. More time needed supposedly.

DT- Not really, they might need more time to make sure before they take that big step. 💍☐

RV- I respect your sentiments but when a woman rejects a marriage proposal,9/10 he's not the one meaning this topic have come up before about marriage, finance, kids career etc. So, I would say coming from a man that was married 20 years together 24 and now divorce. He needs to kick rocks and keep it pushing.

KC- That always depends on the situation.

CG- Depends on who and why.

KS- No. Just not the right time in the relationship. Too soon.

DW- Nope! If I can still get some we can be friends cause I'm not asking again.

KING-ISMS

I'll tell U the DENTIST story:

Letting go is like pulling a tooth. When it is pulled out, you are relieved. But how many times does your tongue run itself over the spot where the tooth was? Probably a hundred times a day. Just because it wasn't hurting you doesn't mean you didn't notice it. It leaves a gap and sometimes you see yourself missing it terribly. It's going to take a while, but its takes time. Should you have kept the tooth? No, because it was causing you too much pain.

Therefore, move on and let go. Consider yourself lucky, as a clear rejection is always better than a fake promise. So, move on. :-)

I Don't Have the Answers, But I Do Have Some Questions

Your Answer

Made in the USA
Columbia, SC
26 June 2018